# What To Do When You Get Hacked

*What To Do When You Get Hacked: A Practitioner's Guide to Incident Response in the 21st Century* teaches you everything that you need to know about preparing your company for a potential data breach. We begin by talking about what the latest cybersecurity threats and attacks are that your company needs to be prepared for. Once we establish that, we go into the different phases of the incident response lifecycle based on the NIST framework. This will teach you how to properly prepare and respond to cybersecurity incidents so that you can be sure to minimize the damage and fulfill all of your legal requirements during a cyber-attack. This book is meant for the everyday business owner and makes these concepts simple to understand and apply.

**Shimon Brathwaite** is author and editor-in-chief of securitymadesimple.org, a website dedicated to teaching business owners how to secure their businesses and helping cybersecurity professionals start and advance their careers.

Before starting his career in Cybersecurity, Shimon was a co-op student at Ryerson University in Toronto, Canada, where he got a degree in Business Technology Management before deciding to specialize in Cybersecurity. Through his work at Ryerson University and his work after graduation, he has accumulated over 5 years of work experience in Cybersecurity across financial institutions, startups, and consulting companies. His work has primarily been in incident response and helping companies resolve security incidents, which is where he learned that most security incidents are caused by only a handful of problems. This is the premise for the book that you are about to read.

If you want to continue to get cybersecurity tips and tricks for free and know when his next book comes out, please visit his website at https://www.securitymadesimple.org/, where you can find new content weekly.

# What To Do When You Get Hacked

## A Practitioner's Guide to Incident Response in the 21st Century

Shimon Brathwaite

CRC Press
Taylor & Francis Group
Boca Raton London New York

CRC Press is an imprint of the
Taylor & Francis Group, an **informa** business

First edition published 2023
by CRC Press
6000 Broken Sound Parkway NW, Suite 300, Boca Raton, FL 33487-2742

and by CRC Press
4 Park Square, Milton Park, Abingdon, Oxon, OX14 4RN

© 2023 Shimon Brathwaite

CRC Press is an imprint of Taylor & Francis Group, LLC

ISBN: 978-1-032-20607-3 (hbk)
ISBN: 978-1-032-20608-0 (pbk)
ISBN: 978-1-003-26429-3 (ebk)

DOI: 10.1201/9781003264293

Typeset in Minion Pro
by SPi Technologies India Pvt Ltd (Straive)

# Contents

# CHAPTER 1

# What Is the Cybersecurity Epidemic?

This chapter will highlight the current state of cybercrime and the amount of damage that it is causing to businesses. There's a cyberattack approximately every 39 seconds and the total global damage of cybercrime is over $20 billion. This chapter will explain to readers why it's important to protect their businesses now more than ever.

## WHY IS CYBERSECURITY SUCH A BIG DEAL?

Cybersecurity has become one of the biggest concerns of any business that operates over the internet. The global damage of cybercrime is now over $20 billion [1] and it has passed the drug trade as the most profitable illegal business in the world. It's estimated that there is a cyberattack every 39 seconds [2]. If your business has a website, web, or mobile application you can expect that this application is being scanned daily by bots or human hackers that are looking for ways to hack into your business. Unlike other forms of crime where people can be restricted by physical location and access, cybercrime takes advantage of the internet's global reach. This means a company can be hacked by anyone, anywhere in the world. Not only this, but many hackers are careful to primarily target businesses and citizens in countries that do not have extradition treaties with their home country, this means that even if law enforcement has a solid lead on who is responsible for a cyberattack, many times they aren't able to take action. They do this usually by programming their malware to search for certain settings on your computer such as default language or location and if the user is in a country that may result in the hacker being prosecuted the malware will simply cease to function. As a result most incidents of companies being hacked result in no action being taken by law enforcement. Less than 1% [3] of cybercrimes see any law enforcement action taken against the hackers and only about 15% of victims even bother to report their cybercrimes to the FBI according to 2016 FBI's Internet Crime Complaint Center (IC3) [4]. The primary reason most people don't report these crimes was "What's the point?". Most people understand that many times the FBI or any other law enforcement agency won't be able to take action unless it's an extremely important situation so they simply don't bother reporting it. Even if your company is one of the lucky 1% where the FBI does want to help and decides to take action. They still face several challenges that make it unlucky that the person will be brought to justice. We talked about jurisdiction a little bit above but another difficulty is simply gathering evidence. Just like physical evidence, digital evidence can be tampered with, erased, and destroyed. If someone makes a mistake as simple as turning off a computer after it has been hacked, that can destroy a lot of the evidence that was stored in the computer's memory because what's stored in the computer's memory is lost once the machine loses power. In cybersecurity, we also have something called anti-forensics, which is simply where hackers take time to remove evidence of their actions as part of the hack to ensure that it's as difficult as possible for law enforcement to piece together what has happened. For example, let's look at computer logs as a case study. Computer logs are simply a record of what has happened on a computer, they can tell you what users logged in, what IP addresses are connected to the machine, what activity was done, and so on. One thing hackers will do is delete these logs in order to prevent investigators from having a trail to follow. The overall point here is that law enforcement has tons of hurdles to go through to even begin to prosecute these individuals and even if they are successful that won't undo the damage to your company. So, it's important that businesses take matters into their own hands and have a plan for preventing their company from getting hacked and recovering in the event that they do.

## WHAT DOES ORGANIZED COMPUTER HACKING LOOK LIKE?

Compared to years ago computer hacking has become far more organized and much easier than in previous years. Many hackers organize themselves into groups that can either be simply for-profit or government-backed groups. This gives them access to resources that make them much more efficient and much more difficult to defend against. Even the individual hackers who may want to make money have access to something called malware as a service (MAAS). It is simply a software product that allows people to pay for malware and use it at their discretion to hack into different companies or people for a profit. In previous years if someone wanted to hack into a computer, they would need the expertise to do so and that would act as a barrier of entry, but that's no longer the case. It's easier than ever for someone to become a computer hacker and start making money, which means there are more hackers now than there have ever been before.

## WHAT DOES THIS MEAN FOR THE AVERAGE BUSINESS?

For the normal business, this means that you can't rely on the government or the police to help protect your company from hackers. With only 1% of cybercrimes ever seeing any law enforcement action means that if you get hacked, most likely you will be on your own. This means you need to be diligent in preparing and protecting your company if you plan to have a lot of online assets. If your company has web applications, a cloud infrastructure, a website, or anything that's connected to the internet. The average data breach globally costs about $3.86 million, if you live in the United States this number is close to $8.6 million per data breach [5]. For many companies suffering major outages because of cyberattacks crippling their businesses, one study found that for small- to medium-sized businesses, about 60% of them would go out of business following a data breach [6]. Let's look at all the ways that a cyberattack costs a business money.

### Stock Prices

When a company suffers a data breach you can expect a dip in stock prices, on average a drop of about 7.27% [7]. For larger companies stock prices are typically seen as an indicator of the company's health and it encourages investors to put money into the company, so this is definitely something you want to manage. Some examples of companies' shares that have dropped following a data breach include Yahoo, LinkedIn, and Facebook.

## Suspended Business Operations

Arguably the biggest blow to any business is a prolonged interruption to business operations. There are two main cyberattacks that cause prolonged interruptions, distributed denial of service (DDOS) attacks and ransomware attacks. However, other forms of cyberattacks can also cause outages if they damage IT infrastructure, make a web application/website unavailable, etc. The average time cost in time of a malware attack is roughly 50 days and during ransomware attacks, companies lose roughly $8500 due to downtime [8]. A famous example of this is when hackers were able to bring down Sony's PlayStation Network for almost three months, causing a massive drop in sales of video games, loss of revenue from subscriptions, and causing many players to move to their competitors' Xbox.

## Loss of Customers

This often comes as a direct result of suspended operations, but loss of customers is a big financial negative to cyberattacks. If your company goes through extended periods of having services unavailable or if customer information is leaked and causes them problems, some customers may decide not to do business with you any longer. Many times word of mouth can spread and create a domino effect where just a small group of disgruntled customers can cause a big loss of revenue for a company.

## Compliance Fees

Depending on your company's industry, location and size you will be subject to several compliance requirements around cybersecurity. Firstly, most of these requirements will mandate that you have security software and processes in place to protect your company. So, things like firewalls, security policies, hiring security staff, and doing security awareness training. Second, they usually require you to notify customers and the regulatory authorities whenever a data breach happens within a certain timeframe. Failure to comply with either of these (whether you are aware of your obligations or not) can result in heavy fines of thousands or millions of dollars and, in the worst case, even jail time for company executives.

## Cyber Insurance Costs

Next on this list are cyber insurance costs, like any other insurance you have if you have an incident your cost of insurance goes up because you are seen as a greater risk, especially, if you are deemed to be at fault. In the context of cybersecurity being deemed at fault would be if you didn't have standard security tools or processes in place. What makes this tricky is there isn't a one size fits all definition of standard security practices, it really depends on the vendor.

Lawsuits

Last but not least is lawsuits, if a cyberattack on the company causes damage to any customers, they are well within their rights to take legal action against the company. Take, for example, a healthcare provider, imagine if a hospital gets hacked by ransomware, they can no longer function as normal and a patient dies. If during the investigation it's found that the hack was possible due to company negligence in protecting a server, renewing their antivirus, or any other basic security measure then you could face a big lawsuit. Another potential lawsuit you may face is if the information that is stolen is used in fraud and costs a customer a large sum of money. Any information that the company has is its responsibility to protect.

## RECAP

Cybersecurity has become one of the most profitable illegal businesses in the world, generating billions of dollars in illegal profit. Due to the global reach of the internet, the difficulty of illegal jurisdictions, and the difficulty of computer forensics in many cases, most instances of cyberattacks go without any type of law enforcement prosecution. This means that hackers tend to be encouraged to continue hacking into companies because there is very little deterrent if they hack someone in a country with bad relations with their home country. Not only that, but with the creation of MAAS, the barrier of entry for someone to start hacking into computers for a profit is becoming lower and lower and this is expected to increase the number of hackers and the number of cyberattacks that we see each year. It's more important than ever that companies take matters into their own hands and invest in protecting their companies in order to save money in the long run. As stated earlier, the average price of a single data breach is over $3 million globally and over $8 million in the United States. Many companies (over 60%) that do suffer a data breach will go out of business within six months, so it's something that you need to be prepared for.

# CHAPTER 2

# What Am I Defending My Company from?

Now that we went over why cybersecurity is important, this chapter is going to focus on exactly what you need to protect your company from. There are several types of cyberattacks that people use and hackers are creating new variations of these constantly but at their core, many of the cyberattacks use the same methodology. This chapter will go over the most common ways that businesses are hacked and what assets are usually targeted by hackers.

## SOCIAL ENGINEERING

In cybersecurity, social engineering is the psychological manipulation of people into performing certain actions or giving up confidential information. A common type of social engineering that you will see in cyberattacks is called phishing, which is simply when someone crafts an email that appears to come from a legitimate source in order to trick the receiver into performing a certain action. Social engineering attacks have become one of the popular types of attacks because it exploits the fact that humans are more easily tricked than software. Typically, software does whatever it is programmed to do and nothing more, whereas people can be manipulated to do things that they shouldn't do much more easily. Social engineering is a means to take advantage of the human element of security. Now that we have open source platforms like social media where people

DOI: 10.1201/9781003264293-2

put large amounts of information about themselves online, it's easier than ever for a hacker to go find that information about someone and then create a specialized social engineering attack to fool them.

## Malware

Malware stands for malicious software and it's any type of software that does harm to a computer system. There are several types of malware out there but arguably the most dangerous type that is used on businesses is ransomware. Ransomware is a type of malware that encrypts all of the information on a machine and then demands that the owner pay a ransom to have the information decrypted. It's popular because it's extremely profitable for the attacker. In 2020, the average ransomware payment was $570,000, up 82% from the previous year [9]. What makes ransomware even worse is that paying a ransom doesn't guarantee that you will get your information back. One study found that in 2021, only 8% of companies that paid the ransom got all of their information back and 29% couldn't recover more than half of the encrypted data [10]. That's over half a million dollars paid out to a hacker to get only a portion of your information back.

Another dangerous type of malware is spyware, which is a type of malware that sits covertly on a computer network, collects information from the machine, and sends it back to the malware author. This type of malware can steal your business secrets, customer information, and employee information and because it's designed to do this covertly, you may not even notice it if you don't have proper network monitoring.

## Advanced Persistent Threats

An Advanced Persistent Threat (APT) is a stealthy threat actor that gains access to a computer network and remains undetected for an extended period of time. The goal with this type of threat is they want long-term access to your company's information and systems. Usually, they will steal data from your company on a regular basis for months or even years at a time. This means your intellectual property won't be safe, your customer information won't be safe, your systems will be one to sabotage at any given time and you may never even know they are there. These types of attacks tend to be nation-state or state-sponsored hacker groups that have a high level of skill and a significant amount of resources to fund their activities.

## Insider Threats

An insider threat is anyone that is already inside of your company boundaries that willingly or unwillingly cause harm to your company. Unlike the APT that comes from outside the network and finds a way inside, an insider threat is someone like an employee that sits inside of your network and can do harm from the inside. It's not just employees, however, this includes contractors, third-party vendors, recently fired employees, and anyone else that is inside of the company. What makes these threats difficult to defend is that they usually have legitimate access to resources in the company so most of the safeguards that you have to protect against people outside the company will be useless. Insider threats require a specially designed solution to ensure that they don't cause harm to the company.

## WHO ARE THE THREAT ACTORS?

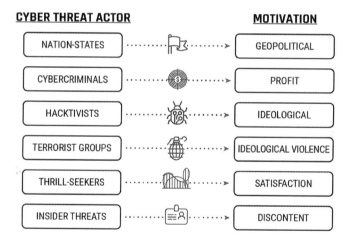

| CYBER THREAT ACTOR | | MOTIVATION |
|---|---|---|
| NATION-STATES | | GEOPOLITICAL |
| CYBERCRIMINALS | | PROFIT |
| HACKTIVISTS | | IDEOLOGICAL |
| TERRORIST GROUPS | | IDEOLOGICAL VIOLENCE |
| THRILL-SEEKERS | | SATISFACTION |
| INSIDER THREATS | | DISCONTENT |

## Types of Hackers

**Cybercriminal:** This a computer security specialist who has extensive computer knowledge and uses it to break into computer systems or networks without the owner's consent, their goal is usually to get some type of financial gain (ransomware), gain information, or do infrastructure damage for Cyber Warfare or just to cause problems for a person or company they do not like (Sony). Black hat hackers are behind the vast majority of computer hacks against large companies. Some black hat hackers don't directly hack into companies, some of them develop computer programs that can be used to hack into a computer and sell it online to other people that are interested in hacking into a certain target. This is often called malware-as-a-service (MAAS) and it provides a safer way for a black hat hacker to make a profit since they aren't directly related to the hacks themselves.

**Nation-State Hacker (State-Sponsored):** These hackers are hired by one government to hack another government, usually to gain information or affect them economically. This group tends to have one of the highest levels of skill because of the complexity of the systems that they are expected to break into. North Korea is one of the most popular examples of countries that invest heavily in state-sponsored hacking groups, and one of their most famous groups is the Lazarus group. North Korea has used computer hacking as a means of generating profit for the country and the United Nations estimates that they made up to $2 billion in 2019 alone [11].

**Hacktivist:** This is a hacker that breaks into a computer system with a politically or socially motivated purpose. They disrupt services to bring attention to their cause and will rarely ever target the everyday civilian. As mentioned earlier, Anonymous is a good example of a group that has been known to use its technical expertise to influence things politically. However, this can include anyone that performs a hack against a company or person in an effort to effect positive change.

**Terrorist Groups:** These are hacker groups that are motivated by some type of ideological goal. Perhaps they think a company is operating unethically and they decide to hack that company in order to put them out of business. Another example may be they believe a country is unethical so they try to hack that company's critical infrastructure and do damage to that country and its people.

**Insiders:** Insiders are people who work within your organization that may do you harm. Insiders can be angry employees, whistleblowers, or contractors. Usually driven by payback, they act to right a wrong that the organization has done to them or their clients. Edward Snowden is a very popular example of an insider who leaked information to the public. While Snowden seemed to do it for a good moral purpose, oftentimes it can be a disgruntled employee simply looking to get back at their company or individuals within the company.

**Thrill Seekers/Script Kiddies:** These individuals are the lowest level of hackers; they don't have very high technical expertise and rely on using pre-written hacking tools to perform attacks. Due to their inability to customize or create malware tools of their own they can be defended against fairly easily by keeping up to date with patching and standard Information Security Best Practices. Script kiddies can perform hacks ethically or unethically but they are separated based on their skill set and how they perform the attacks, which is usually via running someone else's tools.

## WHAT EXACTLY DO THE HACKERS WANT?

The next question that people have when they are learning about cyberattacks is "what do hackers want?". The obvious answer is to hack into the company, the not-so-obvious answer is understanding exactly what type of information hackers want to steal. Not all information is equally valuable for a hacker. Whether they want to offer the company a ransom to get the information back or they are interested in reselling that information on the dark web for money, some information is much more valuable than others. First, you need to understand what the dark web and deep web are. The deep web is a portion of the internet that is not indexed by regular search engines like Google, you can only access this portion of the internet through specialized browsers like TOR and Search Engines like DuckDuckGo. The dark web is a subset of the deep web where illegal activity happens, this can be selling drugs, weapons, and stolen information that can be used for fraud. This is where many hackers take the information that they steal from companies and sell them to get a profit. Now let's look at some of the most valuable information that can be sold on the dark web. When looking at these figures keep in mind that oftentimes hackers will have tens of thousands of these accounts, so even if the price of an individual profile may not be a lot of money when you multiply it by 10,000 or 20,000 it becomes very profitable.

**Financial Information:** Credentials to people's financial accounts as well as transfers from those accounts are one of the most valuable. Some examples of this include banking information, PayPal accounts, transfers from PayPal accounts, credit card numbers with PIN numbers, and just credit card numbers. According to the Dark

Web Price Index 2020, here are some of the prices that you can expect for this type of information.

| Product | Average Dark Web Price (USD) |
|---|---|
| American Express Card with PIN | 35 |
| Cloned MasterCard with PIN | 10 |
| Online banking credentials with at least $2000 USD | 65 |
| Online baking credentials with at least $100 | 35 |
| PayPal transfer between $1000 and $3000 | 320 |
| Stolen PayPal account details, minimum balance $100 | 198.56 |

For whatever reason, transfers from a stolen account tend to go for more money than the actual accounts. This is just speculation but it may be because the person can have more plausible deniability if someone simply transfers the money to them rather than having to log in to the account and move the money from the stolen account.

**Social Media Accounts:** Social Media accounts are another popular item for hackers to steal, especially if they have a high follower count. One reason for this is that the more followers or contacts the person has, the more people the hacker targets with social engineering attacks. By impersonating the legitimate owner of the account the hacker will have a certain level of trust with each of the contacts of that account and therefore their social engineering attack will be much more effective. A little less relevant to this conversation but hackers also tend to sell things like followers and likes on the dark web. Here is a breakdown of how much these accounts go for on the dark web.

| Product | Average Dark Web Price (USD) |
|---|---|
| Hacked Facebook Account | 74.5 |
| Hacked Instagram Account | 55.45 |
| Hacked Twitter Account | 49 |
| Hacked Gmail Account | 155.73 |
| Instagram Followers ×1000 | 7 |
| Spotify Followers ×1000 | 3 |
| Twitch Followers ×1000 | 6 |
| LinkedIn Followers ×1000 | 10 |
| Instagram Likes ×1000 | 6 |

**Personally Identifiable Information (PII):** PII is a broad term for any information that can be linked to an individual person. This is usually a combination of multiple individual pieces of information. For example, a physical address by itself doesn't constitute PII but if you have a first name, last name, and a physical address, now that information is personally identifiable. This type of information is very useful in committing fraud and it is one of the most important pieces of information that you need to protect. Some of the most valuable pieces of PII are government IDs like driver's licenses, passports, and social security numbers. The most valuable type of PII is a subset called PHI personal health information. The reason it's so valuable is that criminals can use this PHI to commit fraud that will allow them to get access to medical equipment and or medicine that they wouldn't be able to get access to on their own. Once they obtain these medical resources, they can be resold for a good profit. You can imagine how much people would pay for certain drugs as an example.

**Intellectual Property/Business Plans:** The last item on this list is going to be business-focused. It's easy to forget that business is a competition, your competitors want to know what's going on in your business so that they can decide on a plan to steal your customers and build a competitive advantage over you. It's difficult to quantify how much this stolen IP is sold for because it's not something that is posted publicly but you can be sure that big corporations are willing to pay for insider information about their competitors. This may not even be from a hacker, this may simply be from an employee (insider threat) within your company that is willing to sell that information to a competitor for a profit.

This isn't an exhaustive list but these are three main categories of information that hackers are looking for when hacking into your company. It's important to keep this in mind because it will help you to understand exactly what you are trying to protect when you invest in your company's cybersecurity program. It's easy to think that you just want to keep hackers out of your network but it's not that simple; they are looking to achieve a specific objective and to properly protect that, you need to have a clear understanding of what is at stake.

## RECAP

As a business owner, you have many information assets that hackers would love to get a hold of to make a profit. It's important that you have a solid understanding of who is after that information and the most common techniques they use to extract that information. When it comes to who wants to hack you, the main culprits will be people looking to make a profit, state-sponsored hackers looking for valuable information, and insider threats who may be looking to make a profit or just get back at you for a perceived wrongdoing. When it comes to the type of attacks you will see, the most popular attack type is social engineering, which takes advantage of the human element of your company. The most popular cyberattack is ransomware, which is designed to force companies to pay a ransom to get their information back, which usually amounts to roughly $570,000. Outside of this, hackers usually gain to steal information that can be used to make a profit by either selling that information or committing fraud in some way or another. The ultimate goal for the business is to protect the company's information as well as its IT infrastructure.

# CHAPTER 3

# How to Get Started with Your Cybersecurity Program

This chapter will introduce the first steps of planning out your company's cybersecurity program. Some of the requirements would be understanding what your company's information assets are, compliance requirements, and the type of product your company is offering. This chapter will give people a framework for assessing what you need to understand and take inventory of before starting your cybersecurity program.

## WHAT IS A CYBERSECURITY PROGRAM?

A cybersecurity program is a documented set of your organization's information security policies, procedures, guidelines, and standards. Simply put, it's everything that governs how your company will approach protecting your company's digital assets. The main goal of a cybersecurity program is to achieve the goals set out in the CIA triad.

Source: @ preferreditgroup.com [13]

DOI: 10.1201/9781003264293-3

CIA stands for confidentiality, integrity, and availability. These are the three goals that you are trying to accomplish.

**Confidentiality:** Confidentiality means that only people with the right access should be able to access any piece of information. In this section of the CIA triad, the focus is on implementing proper security controls that will prevent unauthorized access to your company's resources. A common example of a control that is used to maintain confidentiality is requiring a username and password. The idea being that only the authorized person will be able to provide the credentials and get access to that resource.

**Integrity:** Integrity means that only people with the correct access should be able to change or edit any piece of information, integrity seeks to make sure that the information is always accurate. Integrity is all about making sure that the information that is being used within the company can be trusted to be accurate and free of manipulation. A common example of a security control used to ensure integrity is the use of a digital signature. In a communication between two people, this tool takes a hash value of the original document that can only be decrypted and read by the receiver. The receiver can generate a hash value for the message and if it matches the hash value that they decrypted, then they know the message has not been changed in transit.

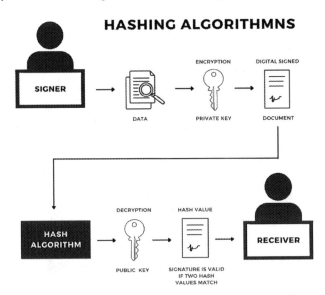

Source: @ Comodo SSL Store [14]

**Availability:** Availability means that you want to ensure that information and services are always available for use by the right user. Think about a company website for example, as a business you want to ensure that this is always up and available for customers to come and interact with your company. However, cyberattacks such as DDOS attacks make these services unavailable and can cost businesses thousands or millions of dollars. A common example of a security control that helps to maintain availability is next-gen firewalls or specialized DDOS protection software.

**Non-repudiation:** There is also a fourth term that isn't included in the triad, but it is associated with the first three. This one is called non-repudiation, simply this means that no one should be able to perform an action online and then deny that they performed this action. For example, if I send an email or delete a file, there needs to be proof that I performed this action so that I can't deny it at a later date.

Everything that you implement in your cybersecurity program should come back to at least one of these four objectives. Ideally, you want to implement things that help with more than one of these areas at the same time but sometimes it may be a good idea to invest in specialized solutions that focus on just one area.

## HOW TO GET STARTED CREATING YOUR CYBERSECURITY PROGRAM?

**Identify All of Your Information:** The first thing you need to do to get started designing your program is to identify all of your digital information. Specifically, all of your sensitive information. In cybersecurity, the keyword is personally identifiable information (PII), which is any information that can be linked to an individual person. Whether it's financial information like customer payment information or health information like patient health records you need to be aware of all of the PII that is on your network. You should also be aware of any company-specific information such as Intellectual Property, trade secrets, future company plans, etc. All of this information is important and can do the company harm if it is leaked outside of the company.

**Identify Where the Information Is Stored:** Once you know what information you have on your network the next step is to figure out exactly where that information is stored. You need to figure out what database it is in, does it live on spreadsheets or files outside of that database, what physical server is it stored on, etc. You can't protect the information if you don't know where it is. Understanding where the information is will be important in understanding what security controls you have to protect it and what controls you need to add to ensure it is safe.

**Take an Inventory of All the Hardware and Software Devices on Your Network:** This is important because every hardware and software device represents a potential vulnerability in your system. Pretty much every mainstream product has security bugs in them and throughout its lifespan patches will be released to fix these vulnerabilities. If you don't have a way of tracking how many of these devices are on your network, you won't be able to apply these patches across your network and you will have vulnerabilities that you aren't even aware of.

**Identify Which Employees Work in Critical Areas:** Cybersecurity is not just about technology, there is a big human element to cybersecurity. Social engineering attacks and phishing attacks in particular are extremely popular methods of hackers breaching a company. If you want to have a strong cybersecurity program you need to make sure your employees are well trained. This includes IT staff, any employees that handle sensitive information, and ultimately every employee in your company needs a basic level of security awareness training.

**Understand Your Compliance Regulations:** Compliance regulations are another important part of planning for your cybersecurity program. Depending on your industry and geographic location there are compliance regulations that will mandate that you have certain security controls in place. You need to be aware of these things to ensure that your cybersecurity program covers all of the required elements for your business's compliance needs.

**Establish Your Budget:** In order to properly plan out your program, you need to understand how much money you have to work with.

There are a lot of costs associated with building out a cybersecurity program. It's not just a matter of hiring people, you also need to consider buying software licenses, buying hardware, and outsourcing certain areas of cybersecurity that would be more cost-effective or perform better through outsourcing than keeping it in house.

**Look at Your Product Offerings:** The last item for this list is to look at your company's product offerings. If your company has a mobile app, for example, you will have different security requirements than a company that doesn't. This information will be used late in a process called threat modeling, where you look at the most common attack vectors that can be used against your company.

## TYPES OF SECURITY CONTROLS

One thing you need to understand when planning out your cybersecurity program is the type of security controls you can use to protect your company.

### Control Categories

**Physical Controls:** This includes all tangible/physical devices that are used to prevent or detect unauthorized access to company assets. This means things such as fences, surveillance cameras, guard dogs, and physical locks and doors.

**Technical Controls:** This includes hardware and software mechanisms that are used to protect assets from non-tangible threats. This includes things like encryption, firewalls, antivirus software, and intrusion detection systems (IDS).

**Administrative Controls:** This refers to the policies, procedures, and guidelines that outline company practices in accordance with security objectives. Some common examples of this will be employee hiring and termination procedures, equipment and internet usage, physical access to facilities, and separation of duties.

### Preventative Controls

A preventative security control is what you use to prevent a malicious action from happening. This will typically be the first type of control you want and when working correctly provides the most effective overall protection. Some examples of this include the following:

**Computer Firewalls (Technical):** A firewall is a hardware or software device that filters computer traffic and prevents unauthorized access to your computer systems.

**Antivirus (Technical):** This is a software program that prevents, detects, and removes malware from computer systems. If you've worked in any corporate environment you have probably noticed this on almost every laptop in the company.

**Security Guards (Physical):** Security guards are typically assigned to an area and they are responsible for ensuring that people do not go into a restricted area unless they can prove they have a right to be there.

**Locks (Physical):** This refers to any physical lock on a door that prevents people from entering without having the proper key. This is important for protecting server rooms from unauthorized access as well as keeping people from entering the premises without proper permission.

**Hiring and Termination Policies (Administrative):** During the hiring process, things like background checks help to prevent people that have a history of bad behavior (e.g., sexual violence) from coming into the company. Termination policies allow managers to get rid of people that are causing problems for the company.

**Separation of Duties (Administrative):** Separation of Duties means requiring more than one person to complete any task. It prevents people from committing fraud because every process requires multiple people and any individuals trying to commit fraud would be noticeable to the other people responsible for carrying out the process.

## Detective Controls

Detective controls are meant to find any malicious activities in your environment that got past the preventative measures. Realistically, you're not going to stop all of the attacks against your company before they happen, so you need to have a way to find out when something has failed and then you can go correct it. Some examples include:

**Intrusions Detection Systems (Technical):** IDS monitor a company's network for any signs of malicious activities and send you alerts whenever an abnormal activity is found.

**Logs and Audit Trails (Technical):** Logs and audit trails are essentially records of activity on a network or computer system, by reviewing these logs you can find out if malicious activity happened on the computer or network.

**Video Surveillance (Physical):** This means having cameras set up in important areas of the company and having people monitor those feeds to see if anyone that isn't supposed to be there was able to get access.

**Enforcing Staff Vacations (Administrative):** Enforced vacations help to detect fraud by forcing individuals to leave their work and have someone else pick up that process. If someone has been doing a fraudulent activity, it will be apparent to the new person that is performing that task.

**Review Access Rights (Administrative):** By reviewing an individual's access rights, you can see who has access to resources that they shouldn't and you can review who has been accessing those resources.

## Deterrent Controls

These attempts to discourage people from doing activities that will be harmful to your company. This way you have fewer actual threats to deal with, usually, this is done by making it harder to perform the action or making the consequences for getting caught well known. Some examples include:

**Guard Dogs (Physical):** Having guard dogs can be intimidating to potential trespassers and helps to deter people.

**Warning Signs (Physical):** By advertising that your property is under video surveillance and has security alarms, it can deter people from trying to break in.

**Pop-Up Messages (Technical):** Having messages displayed on users' computers or corporate homepages warning people of certain behaviors (e.g.. not watching porn on a company laptop).

**Firewalls (Technical):** You may have experienced that when you try to browse certain sites on a corporate laptop you get blocked and a warning message that certain sites are not permitted on the laptop. These messages help to deter people from trying to browse certain sites on company laptops.

**Advertise Monitoring (Administrative):** Many companies make it known that admin account activities are logged and reviewed, this helps to deter people from using those accounts to do bad things.

**Employee Onboarding (Administrative):** During onboarding, you can highlight the penalties for misconduct in the workplace and this helps to deter employees from engaging in bad behavior.

### Recovery Controls

These controls try to get your systems back to a normal state following a security incident. Some examples include:

**Re-Issue Access Cards (Physical):** In the event of a lost or stolen access card, they need to be deactivated and a new access card issued.

**Repair Physical Damage (Physical):** In the event of a damaged door, fence, or lock, you need to have a process for getting it repaired quickly.

**System and Data Backups (Technical):** You should be doing regular backups of important information and have a process in place for quickly restoring to a last known good backup, in the event of a security incident.

**Patching (Technical):** In the event of a new vulnerability coming out that puts your company in an at-risk state, you should be sure to have a process for quickly getting a patch pushed out and returning to a "secure state".

**Disaster Recovery Plan (Administrative):** This is a plan that outlines how to get back to a normal state of operations following a natural or human-made disaster.

**Incident Response Plan (Administrative):** An incident response plan outlines the steps you can take to go back to normal business operations following a cybersecurity breach.

## RECAP

The beginning of a good cybersecurity program comes from proper planning and taking an inventory of what you have within your organization. You need to know exactly what type of PII you have in your company, where it is being held, and have a full inventory of the software and hardware solutions in your company. You also need to understand what your compliance regulations are and make plans to train all of your employees within the company depending on their job role. Once you have all of this information and you understand the different types of security controls that exist, you can begin putting your cybersecurity program together.

# CHAPTER 4

# Why Do You Need Cyber Insurance?

This topic introduces the topic of cyber insurance. Cyber insurance is any type of insurance that covers the costs associated with suffering a data breach. This can include things like paying the ransom for ransomware, physical damage to machines, loss of business, etc. Here, I will discuss the different types of cyber insurance, how it works and why it's so important for a business.

Cyber insurance is a very important thing that is often overlooked when it comes to a company's cybersecurity posture. People are used to getting insurance for all types of life/business-altering events such as a death in the family, medical insurance, car insurance, etc. However, many business owners don't know that they can pay for cyber insurance to protect themselves in the event of a cyberattack that does major damage to their business. Let's look at what exactly cyber insurance can cover.

## WHAT IS CYBER INSURANCE?

Cyber insurance is a specialty line of insurance that covers both businesses and individuals from internet-based risks. Cybersecurity attacks aren't covered in traditional insurance policies.

DOI: 10.1201/9781003264293-4

## WHAT DOES CYBER INSURANCE COVER?

Cyber insurance typically includes first-party coverage against many of the losses associated with hackers. This includes the following:

- Data destruction
- Extortion
- Theft
- Hacking
- Denial of service attacks
- Liability coverage for damage done to other companies
- Regular security audits
- Post-incident public relations
- Investigative expenses
- Criminal reward funds, for example, paying ransoms
- Notifying customers about a data breach
- Credit monitoring for affected customers

## WHAT ARE THE TYPES OF CYBER INSURANCE?

Unfortunately, there's not one type of cyber insurance that covers all of these areas. So you're going to have to evaluate your own risks and see what type of insurance makes the most sense for your company. Here are some of the common ones to consider:

**Network Security:** This insures you against cyberattacks and hacks. This is the broadest and wide-ranging type of insurance. This is what most people will think of when they hear about cyber insurance.

**Theft and Fraud:** Covers destruction or loss of your data as a result of a criminal act or fraud. It also covers the illegal transfer of funds.

**Forensic Investigation:** Covers the Legal, Technical, and Forensic work necessary to determine whether a cyber incident has occurred, to assess the impact of an incident, or determine how to stop an ongoing cyber incident.

**Business Interruption:** This covers lost income and any business costs incurred due to a cyber event.

**Extortion:** This covers costs associated with investigating threats of cyberattacks against the policyholder's systems. It also covers payments to extortionists who threaten to take, delete or disclose company information. A common example of this would be payouts to hackers following a ransomware attack.

**Reputation Insurance:** This provides protection against reputation attacks/cyber defamation. This is usually necessary if the hackers publish confidential information after a successful data breach.

**Computer Data Loss and Restoration:** This covers physical damage to computer-related assets and the retrieving and restoration of data, hardware, software, and other information lost as a result of a cyberattack.

**Information Privacy:** Covers liabilities from actual or alleged noncompliance to information privacy regulations. It also includes legal fees like a defense attorney or monetary settlement.

## WHAT TO LOOK FOR WHEN BUYING CYBER INSURANCE

Like any business insurance, cyber insurance premiums and coverage vary by insurer and the type of policy you choose. You want to make sure you outline your company's main pain points and choose a policy that covers you on those key items. Here are some key tips you can use:

**Understand Your Deductibles:** You want to understand how much you are obligated to pay during an incident. Some people may make the incorrect assumption that insurance covers all of the costs but that's not true, you will be required to cover some of the costs yourself.

**Know How Coverage Applies to Both First and Third Parties:** This applies to your third-party service providers as well as any companies to whom you are a third-party service provider.

**Coverage:** Ask if the policy covers you for any attack you are a victim of or only targeted attacks against your company. This is an important distinction because often you will get infected with malware or some other type of hack that was not specifically directed at your company.

In a way, you are collateral damage and you want to make sure you are covered in these situations as well.

**Understand if the Policy Includes Timeframes for Coverage:** Advanced Persistent Threats (APTs) can last months or years so you need to know if you will be covered if you discover one after a long period of time on the network.

Know if the policy covers non-malicious actions by employees (negligence)

Does the policy cover social engineering?

Does it cover credit monitoring for affected individuals?

**Compare to Other Insurers:** In order to get the best coverage and premiums, you need to shop around. Every insurer is different so take time to find the one that best provides what you need.

## HOW DO CYBER INSURERS ASSESS COMPANIES?

Like all other forms of insurance, insurers want to deal with companies that are low-risk. Therefore, they will do an assessment of your company based on multiple factors. Some of these factors are within your control while others are not. What they find during their assessment will affect the coverage and premiums of your insurance. Here are some of the factors you will be assessed on:

**Security Posture:** The security practices and controls that your organization has in place to reduce the risk of a security breach. The more secure your company is perceived the less of a risk the insurer will deem you and this will influence the prices that you have to pay to get insured. To prove this it's good to have things like a documented layout of your company network, records of past security assessments done, etc.

**Security Policies:** These are the outlines that define what it means to be secure for an organization. They are essentially your internal standards for security within your company. The better these standards are and the more you can prove that you are living up to these standards the less of a risk your business will be considered.

**Annual Gross Revenue:** Another metric that insurers will use to assess you is your company's annual gross revenue. This is important because your financial health will dictate a few things related to cybersecurity. The more money you make the bigger of a target you may be for hackers because there is more incentive for them to breach you. Also, some insurance companies may want to be sure that you have money to pay them consistently and may run the equivalent of a credit check for your company. If your company has a bad history of making payments then you may be denied insurance or you will have to pay a higher rate than a company with a good payment history.

**Types of Services Provided:** Some services are simply bigger risks for cyber-related incidents than others. For example, if you're a cloud service provider where your entire business model is centered around hosting IT infrastructure, then there is a good chance that at some point or another malware will find its way onto one of the systems you're responsible for. Compare this to a business that is primarily a brick-and-mortar business that simply has a website that they want to have insurance for. The more likely the services you offer are to suffer some type of cyber-related incident, the more expensive it will be to get insurance.

**Industry:** Another big factor for the risk of a company to get hacked is the industry that they operate in. Some of the most popular targets for hackers are in the financial industry, healthcare, government, and educational institutions. If your business is in any of these industries, you may be considered a high-risk client to insure and you may have higher costs as a result of that. You can also be affected by the industry that your third-party vendors and business partners are working in. Hackers like to take advantage of trust relationships between companies to move from one business to another. If you are affiliated with high-profile targets that may make you a target for hackers that want to get access to those companies. This increases your overall risk profile and will make your cyber insurance more expensive.

**Data Risk and Exposures:** The last thing they are going to look at is the risk of the data that your company owns. The main target of a hacker when they are trying to breach a company is to steal company information. The type of data that your company collects is going to be a factor in how much of a target you are for hackers. For example, personal health information (PHI) is a very popular target for hackers so if your company collects this information it will make you be seen as a higher risk to insurance companies.

## HOW TO MAKE A BUSINESS CASE FOR CYBER INSURANCE

Security breaches can have a big financial impact on companies, on average it costs companies $3.9 million per data breach [15]. While bigger companies may be content with paying these expenses as they occur, for smaller companies, this is not feasible. In 2016, an article by CNBC found that 43% of all attacks were targeted at small businesses [16]. For larger companies, the average costs of a data breach are still a big impact and having the proper cyber insurance can reduce those costs, allowing for that money to be used for another aspect of business.

Also, cyber insurance is quite expensive compared to the cost of an actual data breach. Cyber insurance in the United States costs roughly $1485 per year on average, that's less than most people's car insurance [17]. Obviously, if you're a bigger company that requires more coverage than this, cost will be higher but the point is that it's much cheaper than taking the chance of getting hacked and having to pay that bill by yourself. Roughly 60% of small- to medium-sized businesses that suffer a data breach close within 6 months of that data breach, based on that alone I think it's worth the investment.

Another way you can pitch for this is to try to bundle this insurance with other insurance that your company already owns. Most businesses will have several types of insurance and it's a well-known fact in the insurance industry that if you combine your insurance policies under one insurer you can get a discount on the price. This will help to lower your overall expense and make it easier to pitch for this in your business. At only $1485 per year, that's already quite cheap for a business and most often, cost is not the reason why companies don't have cyber insurance; many companies simply don't know that it exists.

## RECAP

Cyber insurance is a specialty type of insurance that offers companies financial assistance for many of the costs related to a data breach. It can help with disruptions to business operations, damage to company infrastructure, damage to the company's reputation, and providing aid to affected customers. The cost of cyber insurance is often significantly cheaper than paying to recover from a data breach. Most business own-ers don't even consider getting cyber insurance, but if you expect your company to be around for years to come, investing in cyber insurance is one of the simplest things you can do to prevent irreversible damage to your company. All you need to do is take time to familiarize yourself with the different types of cyber insurance and what they cover and if you ever experience a cyberattack, you will have the peace of mind to know that no matter what happens you will the means to pay for the damages and keep your business up and running.

# CHAPTER 5

# Compliance Regulations You Need to Be Aware of

Compliance regulations dictate the type of security controls that you need to have in place, how your data needs to be handled, and the corrective action that needs to be taken in the event of a data breach. It's important that readers are aware of the major compliance regulations and what the implications of those are for your business's cybersecurity operations.

Compliance is when you need to conform to a rule; in this case, a specific law/regulation. When it comes to your cybersecurity program, compliance regulations will mandate the minimum security and privacy components that your program will need to have.

SECURITY IS PRIMARILY ABOUT ensuring that the company's information is protected from unauthorized access from external sources; data privacy has more to do with making sure that user data is handled properly internally.

Privacy refers to making sure that data is used properly, this means making sure that only the authorized people have access to see data and making sure that this information can't be traced back to any individual person. Typically, once the information can't be linked to any individual person and it's used in accordance with business practices, user privacy will be maintained.

DOI: 10.1201/9781003264293-5

## WHY IS MEETING COMPLIANCE IMPORTANT?

One of the first things people think when they hear compliance is "I understand that the law exists but why should I care? What happens if I'm not compliant?". That's a very valid question; in the past years, compliance regulations have existed but there wasn't as much reason to pay close attention to them. Cyberattacks were much rarer, the requirements were significantly lower and the penalties weren't as bad. However, there are several reasons why you should take meeting your compliance seriously in 2021. Here are some of them:

**Fines, Penalties, and Jail time:** This is the first and most obvious reason you want to make sure you are compliant. Businesses pay millions of dollars per year due to being non-compliant. One of the most aggressive when it comes to charging fines is GDPR; they have collected over $63 million in fines in the first year that it was introduced [18]. Google alone has been charged with a $57 million fine for unclear data harvesting practices [19].

**Cyberattacks Have Become More Common:** It's estimated that there is a new cyberattack every 39 seconds. At this point, you need to expect that your company is going to face multiple cyberattacks per year, whether it's manual or from a computer bot. If you suffer a data breach and upon investigation, if it's found that you weren't in compliance, then the negative consequences of the hack will be compounded with the penalties of the regulatory body whose legislation you didn't comply with. The odds of you being able to stake under the radar so to speak are decreasing.

**Companies Have More Data Than Ever:** The amount of online information that companies collect has increased significantly in the last decade. It's estimated that users create 2.5 quintillion bytes of data every day [20]. Most of this information is created or collected by businesses. Every piece of information comes with a set of requirements when it comes to getting consent, processing, etc. Given how much information is being collected it's easy to make mistakes if you're not clear on what your compliance requirements are.

**You Can Lose Business:** If you do B2B business, your ability to demonstrate compliance with industry standards and regulations is often a requirement to do business with certain companies. Even if your company doesn't have the requirement, if you want to handle information from other businesses as part of a contract, you need to be able to demonstrate that you understand and will uphold their compliance requirements. The reason being is that the company that collected and owns the data is ultimately responsible for ensuring compliance of their third-party vendors so they will have a vested interest in making sure that the requirements are met.

Depending on the type of business that you run and the size of the company, you will have compliance regulations that mandate that you handle customer information in a certain way. This includes having the proper security controls, anonymizing customer information, getting customer consent, and many other requirements. As a startup founder, you need to be aware of these requirements or you can run the risk of getting heavy fines or even having your business's operations suspended. Here are some of the main regulations you should be aware of:

**PCI-DSS:** PCI-DSS stands for payment card industry data security standard. In September 2006, five major credit card brands (Visa International, MasterCard, American Express, Discover, and JCB) established the payment card Industry Security Standards Council (PCI-SSC). PCI-SSC created and continues to oversee PCI-DSS, which is an information security standard for organizations that accept or process credit cards in any way. Failure to comply with the rules outlined in this standard can result in heavy penalties. For example, one Tennessee-based retailer was charged $13.2 million by Visa for failure to meet the standards [21]. Typically, fines range from 5k to 10k per month until compliance is achieved, but these fines increase the longer a company doesn't meet compliance [22]. Also, fines ranging from $50 to $90 can be charged per affected customer if a data breach occurs.

**CCPA:** The California Consumer Privacy Act (CCPA) gives California residents more control over the personal information that businesses collect on them. CCPA applies only to for-profit businesses that do business in California (regardless of where your headquarters is) and meet any of the following requirements:

Have a gross annual revenue of over $25 million.

Buy, receive, or sell the personal information of 50,000 or more California residents, households, or devices.

Derive 50% or more of their annual revenue from selling California residents' personal information.

Please Note: It doesn't apply to non-profit businesses or government agencies.

CCPA fines a maximum civil penalty of $2500 for every unintentional violation and $7500 for every intentional violation of the law [23].

**GDPR:** GDPR stands for General Data Protection Regulation and it is a privacy law set out by the European Union (EU). It became effective as of May 25th 2018. Even though it was set out by the EU, it affects all companies that collect information for citizens of the EU. Ernst & Young estimated that the world's 500 biggest corporations are on track to spend up to $7.8 billion on GDPR compliance [24]. As of January 2020, GDPR has led to over $126 million in fines, with the biggest fine being 50 million euros paid out by Google. GDPR fines **up to €20 million ($24.1 million) or 4% of annual global turnover** (whichever is higher) [25].

## GDPR ENFORCEMENT

- In total, there were *$63 million* of fines issued in the first year of the GDPR.

- Google was hit with a fee of *$57 million* for unclear data harvesting practices.

- There have been *144,000 complaints* filed with various GDPR enforcement agencies and *89,000 data breaches* recorded. 37% are still pending investigation of penalties.

SOURCE: @VARONIS [26]

**HIPAA:** HIPAA stands for Health Insurance Portability & Accountability Act and was passed by Congress in 1996. The privacy aspect of HIPAA is overseen and enforced by the US department of health and human services (HHS) office, starting in April 2003. HIPAA does a few different things, but from a compliance point of view it's all about mandating the protection of consumer health information, this is referred to as HIPAA privacy regulation. HIPAA privacy regulation requires health care providers and their business associates to develop and follow procedures to ensure the confidentiality and protection of personal health information (PHI). You can see HIPAA fine information below.

# HIPAA Violation Penalties

| $100 - $50,000 per violation<br>Maximum $25,000 per year | $1000 - $50,000 per violation<br>Maximum $100,000 per year |
|---|---|
| **TIER 1**<br><br>Unaware of the HIPAA violation and by exercising reasonable due diligence would not have known HIPAA Rules had been violated. | **TIER 2**<br><br>Reasonable cause that the covered entity knew about or should have known about the violation by exercising reasonable due diligence. |
| **TIER 3**<br><br>Willful neglect of HIPAA Rules with the violation corrected within 30 days of discovery. | **TIER 4**<br><br>Willful neglect of HIPAA Rules and no effort made to correct the violation within 30 days of discovery. |
| $10,000 - $50,000 per violation<br>Maximum $250,000 per year | $50,000 per violation<br>Maximum $1.5 million per year |

Source: @ HIPAA Journal [27]

**PIPEDA:** The Personal Information Protection and Electronic Document Act (PIPEDA) is a regulatory requirement that applies to private sector organizations that collect personal information in Canada. It's designed to ensure the protection of personal information in the course of commercial business. Compliance requires that you follow 10 fair principles that govern the collection, use, and disclosure of personal information as well as providing access to personal information for customers. PIPEDA fines include up to $100,000 per violation.

**SOX Compliance:** SOX stands for Sarbanes–Oxley Act, passed in 2002, and establishes regulations to protect the public from fraudulent business practices by corporations. It was passed following some large business scandals, where companies like Enron, Tyco, and Adelphia used deceptive business practices to trick the public. In order to protect consumers, it mandates more transparency in the financial reporting of corporations. It requires companies to have formalized checks and balances to ensure that their reporting is accurate. SOX applies to all publicly traded companies in the United States, subsidiaries, and foreign companies that are publicly traded and conduct business within the United States.

When it comes to penalties and fines, SOX specifically penalizes the corporate officer (usually CEO or CFO) that is responsible for compliance. An officer that doesn't comply or submits an inaccurate certification is subject to a $1 million fine and ten years in prison, even if done accidentally. If an inaccurate account is submitted on purpose the fine can be up to $5 million and 20 years in prison.

**China PDPL (Personal Data Protection Law):** At the time of this book, this regulation has not been finalized, it's currently a first draft but China has committed to creating its very own data privacy law. China's PDPL is structured similarly to other regulations and in particular it's modeled very closely to GDPR. It consists of eight chapters and seventy articles. Here are the main six components that you need to be aware of:

1. **Consent:** This requires that businesses get written permission when gathering information from the citizens of China.

2. **Processing of Personal Information:** Under PDPL all citizens of China have the right to know and make decisions on his/her personal information if they don't like the handling process of the company that collected their information. The only exception to this is if the information is being handled by the state.

3. **International Data Transfer/Cross Border:** This regulation mandates data privacy requirements for any data that leaves the Chinese border. Some examples of this are requiring written consent, informing the individual about the nature of the processing and transfer and passing through a security assessment organized by the state cybersecurity authority and information department. Failure to comply can result in the restriction of transferring data across the Chinese border.

4. **Rights of Individuals (Citizens):** Every citizen in China will be given rights regarding their data privacy that must be upheld by companies within China and internationally, similar to GDPR.

5. **Personal Data Protection:** As the name suggests this legislation is China's first law specifically made to protect the personal information of Chinese citizens and will cover all personally identifiable information (PII).

6. **Liabilities/Penalties:** Where personal information is handled in violation of this law, PDPL will enforce penalties for the offending companies. The Chinese department fulfilling personal data protection duties and responsibilities will order correction, confiscate unlawful income and issue a warning to the company. If the company still fails to comply, it will be subject to fines of not more than 1 million Yuan for the offending company. The directly responsible person and other directly responsible personnel are fined between 10,000 and 100,000 Yuan.

**Australia Data Privacy Act:** In 1988, the privacy act was passed and serves as Australia's primary piece of legislation for protecting the handling of personal information about citizens of Australia. This act applies to all government agencies and private sector organizations that have an annual turnover of $3 million or more. The privacy act is supported by the privacy regulation of 2013 and the privacy (credit reporting) code of 2014.

## RECAP

Compliance regulations are a set of rules that organizations need to adhere to. They are enforced by a regulatory body and can either be national, international, or based on your industry. These rules typically govern how companies can collect information, process it, store it, and often mandate that companies have a baseline level of security and privacy measures in place. Failure to comply with a compliance regulation can have several consequences, the most common are penalties/fines, suspension of a business license, and, in severe cases, jail time.

# CHAPTER 6

# How to Be Prepared for Insider Threats

Insider threats require special preparation because they are already inside of the company and therefore can't be stopped with conventional means. This chapter will introduce the specific controls and processes that you need to have in place to ensure that insider threats can't successfully attack a company from the inside.

N OT ALL THREATS TO your company come from external sources. Insiders are threats to an organization that come from people within a company; such as employees, former employees, contractors, or business partners. According to IBM's 2015 Security Intelligence Index, 31.5% of attacks were by malicious insiders, 23.5% of attacks were by inadvertent insiders and 95% involved someone inside the company making a mistake [28]. The key element is that they have:

1) information concerning the organization's security practices, data, or systems.

2) the means to access and tamper with company assets.

One thing to remember about insider threats is that they can be malicious and non-malicious. A malicious insider is someone that intentionally seeks to sabotage the company in some way. So, for example, think of an employee that sells company secrets or access to the company's

DOI: 10.1201/9781003264293-6

network for a profit. A non-malicious insider threat is someone that unintentionally causes harm to the company. This can be a regular employee that, due to their lack of knowledge of security awareness, clicks on a link in a phishing email and their actions cause malware to be introduced to the environment. Both of these types of threat insiders are very dangerous and can cause issues for your companies, neither is necessarily more dangerous than the other.

Traditional security measures such as firewalls, antivirus, physical checkpoints, and others are designed to protect your company from external threats but are ineffective at protecting you from internal threat actors. In order to reduce this risk, you need to take a different approach. The core idea that will be seen throughout the section below is the idea of zero trust. Simply put, the zero trust model seeks to remove all aspects of trust from an organization's network architecture. This means that every employee that needs access to a specific resource or piece of information needs to demonstrate that they have a business need and they need to authenticate themselves. The reason insider threats can cause so much damage is because the company trusts them and allows them access to resources and information. To prevent this we need to take steps to eliminate that trust wherever possible so that any action taken by an insider threat will be limited in the amount of damage it can cause.

Here, I'll outline some of the key principles and controls you can use to prevent security incidents caused by internal sources:

## THE PRINCIPLE OF LEAST PRIVILEGE

This concept applies to all work and simply means that any employee, contract, or third party should be given the least amount of access and information needed to do their jobs. By minimizing the amount of access and information that people have, it reduces their ability to perform actions that may be damaging to your business.

## SEGREGATION OF DUTIES

Some actions or information are so important that the misuse of either can have a huge impact on the business. One way to protect against this is to use segregation of Duties, which requires that multiple people work together in order to perform a certain task. For example, you shouldn't have the same person approving an order, making the purchase for the order, and doing the review of purchases for your business. If you have the same person doing all these functions, it's too easy for them to misuse money because there is no other person to review what that person is doing.

## MANDATORY VACATIONS

Vacations aren't always just in the interest of the employee. Enforcing mandatory vacations helps to identify misconduct in a business because someone else will be taking over that process while the other person is gone. For example, if someone is able to do a process undisturbed for three years, if they are doing something illegal it will be very hard to know that because no one is directly involved in that process, reviewing that person's work. But if that person is forced to take two or three weeks off and someone else must take over that process, there's a good chance that the person taking over will notice if something was not being done properly. Additionally, it also ensures that there are multiple people trained on how to do any particular task. If only one person is trained to perform a business function, the company can become over-reliant on that person and this can cause problems for the business if that person ever leaves. Mandatory vacations ensure multiple people will be able to perform that function and helps to prevent over-reliance on any one individual.

## DEVELOP A GOOD EMPLOYEE TERMINATION PROCEDURE

Many security problems come from recently fired employees. Obviously, being let go from a company can be a stressful and emotional experience for many people. As a result many people decide to get back at the company. This can mean physical violence against managers or co-workers, destroying company property, destroying company information (through the planting of viruses or destroying documents), and many other means of revenge. According to a study by the CERT Insider Threat Center, about 85% of sabotage cases by disgruntled employees had revenge as the primary motivation [29].

It's important to have a concise plan on how to properly terminate an employee. The key here is to remove access to physical facilities and company networks at the same time to ensure that they can't perform any damaging actions. It's also important to remember to treat people humanely and with respect so that fewer people feel compelled to try and get back at the company.

## HAVE PROPER SURVEILLANCE

This includes monitoring all important areas of your company by video cameras, this is typically done with motion sensors and night vision. It's also important to have signs letting people know they are being watched in these areas to help deter people from doing things they aren't supposed to. Also, you can enable session screen-capture technology on all critical servers and devices owned by highly privileged users. This way you can easily get screenshots to use as evidence in the event of suspicious behavior.

## HAVE PROPER BACKUPS AND RECOVERY PROCESSES

Establishing a policy that regularly creates full backups is a good general practice and helps to ensure that if there is a major security incident, the business can be restored with minimal damage. In policies like these, full backups should be performed at least once a month and incremental backups should be performed at least weekly. This way if a disgruntled employee destroys some information or malware is introduced to the environment you can recover your most important information.

## KEEP TRACK OF EMPLOYEE ACCESS

Privilege Creep is the slow accumulation of unnecessary permissions, access rights, and other privileges by a user as they remain at a company. It happens very often because many times access is granted but not removed, so over time the amount of access a user has will continuously increase. While not ideal, it can be acceptable in some situations, but if that access allows the user too much freedom it should be revoked once it's no longer needed to prevent privilege creep.

## MONITOR YOUR NETWORK FOR SUSPICIOUS ACTIVITY

Using tools like SIEMs, you can monitor your network for suspicious activity by employees. You can implement log management and change auditing software that will look at actions performed across the entire organization. Another important aspect of this is User Behavior Analytics (UBA) technology. This is the technology that detects insider threats, targeted attacks, and financial fraud by looking at patterns of human behavior and then identifying anomalies from those patterns that may indicate a threat to your company. It's another application of machine learning with big data, which helps identify threats within your network.

## HAVE WELL-DEVELOPED POLICIES FOR PROPER USER BEHAVIOR

You should have policies that outline how employees should act during their employment and inform them of what type of monitoring/surveillance your company performs. Some of these related to acceptable standards of behavior should be included in the onboarding process and employment contract. While others should be documented and made available to employees to read or sign as required. The goal here is to make sure that the expectations are established at the beginning of the work relationship. Some common policies that companies have include the following:

- User monitoring policy
- Acceptable use policy
- Third-party access policy
- Workplace conduct policy
- Password management policy

It's important to work with HR and legal teams to ensure that people are made aware of these rules, the consequences of breaking them, and ensuring that all your legal requirements are fulfilled. You also want to make sure that the rules you put in place don't violate any privacy or workplace laws.

## EMPLOYEE TRAINING

Training employees on how to identify suspicious behavior and giving them an anonymous way to report that behavior is critical. You can't be everywhere so encouraging employees to report that behavior and even incentivizing it can be very valuable in helping to identify fraud, abuse, harassment, and all sorts of negative behaviors you don't want.

## SECURITY AWARENESS TRAINING

The last item on this is to implement security awareness training for your employees. While this doesn't do anything to protect against malicious insiders, it can do a lot to reduce the likelihood of non-malicious insiders performing actions that may be harmful to your company. In particular, you should invest in training employees in two areas. The first is to identify social engineering attacks, phishing attacks in particular are the biggest way that employees are used to cause harm to their employers. To combat this training on how to identify and report these types of threats is important. The second is teaching employees how to handle sensitive information securely and maintain user privacy, in particular, how to protect their login information, teaching them not to share information, and how to dispose of information securely. By teaching your employees these best practices, you can make it harder for malicious insiders to get access to valuable company information. This may sound ridiculous but dumpster diving is a common way for people to steal company information. People print off documents with company information, throw it in the garbage, and then someone comes along that's willing to go through the company's garbage and they can find all sorts of useful information on that company.

## RECAP

Insider threats refer to any entity in the company that has internal access to the company. This can be employees, contractors, third parties, etc. These entities pose a special security risk because they are already inside the company's perimeter so many of the standard security measures will not be useful in preventing them from causing harm to your company. It's important that you take steps to prevent damage from both malicious and non-malicious insider threats.

# CHAPTER 7

# How to Build an Effective Incident Response Team

Here, I will go over the different elements needed to hire and build an effective incident response team. To make an effective team you will need a few different job roles, each with different skill sets and specializations if you want to be effective. I'll cover all of these roles and why they're important in this chapter.

## NIST INCIDENT RESPONSE LIFECYCLE

Before we talk about how to build an incident response team we need to discuss something called the incident response lifecycle. Simply put this is a framework for modeling how your IR team will respond in the event of a security incident. For this example, I will use the NIST version of the IR lifecycle.

### Incident Response Lifecycle SP 800-61

This incident response lifecycle is one of NIST's most popular frameworks and is used by many corporations as a means of standardizing the way they respond to security incidents. In this workflow, NIST recommends four steps: 1) Preparation, 2) Detection and Analysis, 3) Containment, Eradication, and Recovery, and 4) Post-Incident Activity. Here, I'll briefly

DOI: 10.1201/9781003264293-7

go over each of these steps so you can understand what your incident response team will be responsible for.

**Preparation:** The first thing you need to do as part of your incident response process is preparation. This is where the incident response team gets prepared for a potential cybersecurity incident. This is where you do things like build out playbooks, hire staff, implement security controls, gather notification requirements and KPIs, etc. It's important that everyone in your organization understands what their responsibilities are in the event of a cybersecurity breach so that you don't have confusion when the incident does occur, because they will. It's also important to understand how your team's performance will be measured. Whether you work in management or as part of the team your performance will be evaluated for things like promotions or to see who will be let go if anyone is and you want to understand what metrics you are being judged by. Some common examples may be the average time to resolve an incident, the average time your security tickets go without an update, etc.

**Detection and Analysis:** Next is the first phase of the actual investigation which is the detection and analysis phase. Typically, detection will be performed by some type of security software like an intrusion detection system (IDS) or a security software like windows defender. Once the alerts are sent to the analysts, the analysis phase begins. In this phase, you are performing the investigation of an alert to see if it is a false positive or a real security incident. If it is found to be a legitimate issue, then you perform an analysis to see the scope of the issue and the potential impact and determine what actions are needed to contain and resolve the issue.

**Containment, Eradication, and Recovery:** In this phase, your first priority is Containment. This means that you first stop the spread of the issue. For example, if you have a computer virus spreading to machines on your network, you want to isolate those machines by taking them off the network so that the virus can no longer spread to another machine. Once you have isolated all the machines on your network the incident has been contained, because it can no longer spread and grow. It's important to do this first because if you start removing viruses from machines while the virus is still spreading on the network it's very difficult to make progress. For every machine that you remove the virus from, another may get infected.

The next phase is Eradication. This simply means getting rid of the problem entirely. Within the context of cybersecurity, this includes two main components. Firstly, you need to remove any signs of infection such as malware or revoke the access from an account that has been compromised so that it no longer poses a risk to the company. The second element of this is that you need to remediate the root cause of the security incident. For example, if a system was compromised because a system was not properly patched then you should apply the appropriate patches in this step of the incident response lifecycle. This ensures that whenever the system is introduced back into the work environment not only will it not pose a threat currently but it should be protected against similar attacks in the future.

The last element of this phase is Recovery. Recovery means restoring the machines to their original state and it includes reintroducing the machine back to the production environment. To do this properly you first need to verify that the machine has been hardened and is no longer vulnerable to the same vulnerability that allowed for the attack. Next, it needs to be integrated back into the environment, many times this will require you to restore the machine's data using the best available backup or re-imaging the machine.

**Post-Incident Activity:** After the incident has been resolved, there is still work for you to do. Many times, you may encounter a security incident that was previously unknown or has a unique root cause. If you found that there wasn't a standard operating procedure (SOP) for any situation that occurred during the incident, that situation should be reviewed and a new process created in this step.

## BUILDING OUT THE INCIDENT RESPONSE TEAM

### Roles and Responsibilities

The first thing you should think of when trying to put together an incident response team is the type of job roles you need to hire. The people you hire and their expertise is the most valuable resource you will have and there are certain core competencies that you need to function well.

**Team Leader:** This is a person or people that will be responsible for coordinating all of the incident response team's activities. For this role, the person doesn't need to have a lot of technical expertise but they should be good at communication and project management.

This person may also be responsible for reporting any important information to the proper stakeholders within the company.

**Communications:** Next, you need someone that can handle communication with outside stakeholders. For example, let's look at data privacy. If you have a security incident that compromises the privacy of a customer's information then that needs to be reported to the appropriate data privacy office. You need someone either on your team or working with the team that can be a subject matter expert on these issues and make sure that you are meeting all of your communication requirements. In addition to communicating with outside stakeholders, you also want someone that can handle all internal communications within the business. You may need to inform employees of a cyberattack or other internal emergency and you don't want your IT staff doing that, you want someone who is trained in communications that knows how to tailor the message and control the narrative to create these messages. Lastly, in the event of something like a ransomware attack, where you need to communicate with hackers and potentially negotiate on behalf of the company, you want someone with expertise in communications to handle that negotiation.

**Technical Investigator:** This serves as the technical expert on the team. When you're doing an investigation you may need to do things like examine log files, do computer forensic work, or extract evidence from a system using security tools. The technical investigator/expert is someone that excels in doing this type of intensive, technical work and can provide support for other analysts where needed. This information will be used to determine the cause of the attack, signs of compromise, lateral movement, and other important indicators in the security incident.

**Analysts/Investigators:** Now these are people that are going to do the bulk of the work for your incident response team. Typically, the way this works is that you have multiple analysts and as potential security incidents come in, they are assigned to individual analysts that will run those investigations and keep the team leader informed on what's happening. These analysts need to have a strong foundational knowledge of cybersecurity as well as the incident response lifecycle so that they can be counted on to run the investigations properly. For very technical components of the investigation, they can leverage the technical investigator for those tasks.

**Legal Counsel and HR:** This may not be apparent at first but you should have legal counsel and someone that is familiar with HR practices consulting the team. While most of your security incidents will be from external threats, insider threats are still a real risk and you're going to need people that can advise you on your internal investigations. For example, you need to know how to handle employees that are suspected of foul play in case you want to press charges, fire them, etc. Legal counsel will be important for informing you of employees' rights as well as the rights of your customers while HR is important for helping to deal with employees.

**Data Privacy:** Whenever there is a successful hack you run the risk of customer data being compromised. There are several laws both local and international that give customers right over the data that has been collected by a business. In that situation the business needs to take steps to ensure that they are in accordance with those laws, inform the proper people and take the steps required to fix the situation. This person may or may not be separate from the legal counsel. Sometimes your company may have a lawyer that specializes in data privacy or they will have someone who is a data privacy specialist.

## Documentation and Playbooks

You don't want to be figuring out how to respond to a security incident while the incident is happening. To avoid this, companies invest in either getting or creating documentation on what their analysts should do in certain situations so that they have a reliable set of steps to follow. Having good documentation prevents people from making mistakes that may endanger the company and makes investigators more efficient on the job. Also, you need to consider the fact that people come and go from your business, and if all of your team's experience and knowledge is stuck in their heads, then it leaves you whenever they leave the company. Good documentation makes it easier for you to transition from one employee to another and, therefore, it will take new employees less time to get up to speed. Here are some of the different types of documentation you should have for your team:

**IR Playbooks:** In the Incident Response (IR) field they have something called IR playbooks, which are essential manuals on how to respond to certain types of security incidents. You should have playbooks on all of the major types of attacks that you expect to encounter. Some examples of this include ransomware, DDOS, a Web Application being down, a malicious employee, and overall malware outbreak. You are free to make these playbooks yourself or you can use playbook templates from established organizations like SANs or NIST. Even if you create a custom solution for your environment, I would suggest you begin by using a template from an established organization.

**Standard Operating Procedures (SOP):** This is simply a step of steps that need to be followed in order to achieve a certain result. While playbooks are generally targeted toward a type of cyberattack, an SOP document can be for any process in the company and has only one process objective in mind. For example, this may be how to create a report in Qualys for all of the machines that are affected by a certain vulnerability. They are relatively short and step-by-step instructions on how to complete the task.

**Contact Sheet:** When you are handling a security incident, there are several people that need to be informed, brought into the investigation, or consulted. All of these key people and their contact information should be collected and stored in a central document. This way, whenever someone needs to be contacted, it will be easy for everyone on the team to find them.

**KPI Documents:** This may not need to be available to the entire team but whoever is managing the team should be well aware of what KPIs the team are being measured on. While the ultimate goal of the team is to resolve security incidents, like any other team, there are going to be specific KPIs by which you are judged and you need to understand them in order to make sure the team is evaluated favorably.

Needless to say, these documents are only as useful as they are well kept. For example, if you have a contact sheet that hasn't been updated in three years, there is a good chance that the contact information will be outdated and therefore not useful in an emergency situation. All of these documents should be updated at least every six months.

## HOW TO INTERVIEW FOR YOUR INCIDENT RESPONSE TEAM

In order to get the best candidates for your team, you need to have a good interview process. If your interview process isn't thorough enough then you run the risk of hiring people that are not capable of doing the job and it will make your job as the team manager a lot more difficult. A survey by CareerBuilder found that 74% of employers admitted to hiring the wrong person and the approximate cost for that wrong hire was roughly $14,900 each [30]. Even if you're not hiring this person with money out of your pocket (because you aren't the business owner), you still don't want to be in a position where you hire someone that can't do the job or is simply a horrible person to work with. They will make your life much harder and if they make it past the probationary period then they may be very difficult to get rid of even if you are in a management position. So here are some tips that you may use to reduce the chances of making the wrong hires:

Ask about Their Process and Why: One mistake interviewers make is to ask definition-based questions, things like what is a threat or a vulnerability. While this information is important it's very easy for someone to simply google common interview questions, do some memorization and repeat that back to you. You want to structure your questions to be more open-ended and allow them to give a thought-out answer that will tell you about how that person thinks as well as the depth of their understanding.

Include a Technical Interview Component: Many companies have started to include a take-home technical assessment for evaluating candidates that they think have potential. I think this is a great idea to see what people can do, especially for very technical roles. The only critique I would give is that you should pay people for their time. Many candidates don't want to spend hours producing their best work if there is no guarantee that it will get them the job. As the employer, you don't want people rushing through the assignment; pay people appropriately for their time so they are incentivized to do their best work and in that way, you can get the best possible candidate.

Look at Their Side Projects: Side projects can tell you a lot about a person. For one someone that is able to maintain a side project over the long term has intrinsic motivation and self-discipline. It's easy for someone to do work when they have someone over them making them do it and holding them accountable, but it's another skill to be a self-starter that can motivate themselves. Also, it can show you how that person thinks and operates. If you ask someone about the work that they did at another company, many times, that process was not their own creation. Whereas if you look at someone's side projects, you can see how they think, and why they do things a certain way and that can tell you a lot about what you can expect of that person in this new position.

**Don't Overvalue Certifications:** While certifications can establish a baseline level of knowledge among candidates within the incident response role, I would suggest that you treat them as optional and not requirements. Some companies will filter out applications that don't have any certifications, but I wouldn't recommend this approach, especially for a junior position.

**Don't Reject Intrapreneurs:** Most people have heard the question "Where do you see yourself in 5/10 years". Some employers get very offended or weary if they hear someone talking about starting a business or going to work for another company. You don't want to reject people just because they don't say they expect to stay at the company for 5–10 years. You want to hire people that are ambitious, hardworking, and have a vested interest in doing well. Many of these people will have the idea of working for themselves one day or going to work for a big-name company. These people may not stay for 10 years but in the time that they are there, they will have a great impact on your company and they will find ways to improve your processes more than someone that's thinking "I want to get this job and just coast with this company". Don't be afraid of someone that is ambitious because you may just be rejecting an intrapreneur that would greatly increase the productivity of your team.

## 30 SAMPLE INTERVIEW QUESTIONS

Here are some interview questions you can use to evaluate candidates as well as roughly the type of answer you are looking for in response.

### Junior Level

These questions are good for any job position where you're looking for someone with 1–3 years of experience: The standard entry-level positions where they will be doing the initial triage of alerts and escalating those to a more senior member of the team.

1) What is the difference between a threat, vulnerability, and risk?
A vulnerability is a weakness in a system or program. A threat is an entity that tries to exploit the vulnerabilities in a system and a risk is the potential loss, damage, or destruction of an asset as a result of a threat exploiting a vulnerability.

2) What is the CIA triad?
The CIA triad is confidentiality, integrity, and availability. Confidentiality means ensuring that only the authorized users have access to information. Integrity means protecting information from unauthorized modifications. Availability means ensuring that information is available to users whenever they request the service. As a bonus, you can ask them about non-repudiation, which is essentially making it so that no user on a system can deny having performed an action on that system.

3) What are some common Indicators of compromise for identifying a compromised system?
This is important because as junior investigators, they will typically be handling a lot of the alerts that come in and escalating the more important ones to Senior Analysts. Therefore, they need to have an understanding of what a genuine instance of infection looks like vs normal processes on a machine. Some common signs of infection are slow performance, high memory usage, lack of storage space, unexpected pop-ups, disappearing or moved files, and your system unexpectedly shutting down.

4) What is a DDOS attack and potential mitigation?
A distributed denial of service (DDOS) attack is an attempt to disrupt normal traffic by spamming a device with unsolicited traffic until the machine can't respond to legitimate traffic. Some common ways of mitigating DDOS are to use packet filtering devices like firewalls, blocking IP addresses that are spamming you, getting DDOS protection as a service, or redirecting the traffic (sinkholing).

5) What security blogs or podcasts do you follow?
Staying up to date with news in security is very important, especially in incident response. There are consistently new vulnerabilities being announced, new patches, potential vendor breaches, and many other elements that require you to be aware of what's going on. Someone

that is involved in the community and staying up to date on these situations will be more valuable in investigations.

6) What is the difference between a false positive and a false negative and which is worse?
A false positive is when an alert is created for an activity that is not malicious, while a false negative is when there is no alert generated for an activity that is malicious. A false negative is worse because that means that malicious activity is going undetected, while a false positive is just more of an inconvenience. It's important that a candidate understand that not all alerts will be security incidents.

7) How does a ping work?
The ping tool is used to test whether a host is reachable over a network. It works by sending a request to that machine and if that machine responds by sending back a data packet, we know that machine can be accessed. This is a fairly simple technical question meant to test their understanding of basic networking concepts.

8) How would you investigate an alert?
Here, you want to see what this person's thought process and understanding of investigating a security incident is. A good answer to this would include looking at things like file names, process names, hash values, URLs, and other behaviors to determine if the alert is based on a malicious activity or not. Other good things would be if they discuss using tools like VirusTotal to verify the information and see if it's worth escalating.

9) What security software have you worked with in the past?
At the junior level, you may not have candidates with a lot of hands-on experience so any experience that they do have whether on the job, in school, or while working on side projects is a plus. It's worth taking time to see what they have worked with in the past and see if they have any experience working with the tools that you use.

10) What made you apply for this position?
Unlike senior positions where the person has a long career in the field and has shown that they want to do this type of work, applicants for junior positions are less of a safe bet. They may be coming out of school with no or little experience in the field and it's hard to know six months down the line if they are going to be punctual,

professional, focused on the overnight shifts, etc. Ideally, you're looking for someone that applied for this job as part of their overall career trajectory and gives you a strong sense that they will be reliable and not just burn out and want to do something different in a short amount of time.

## Mid-Level

For mid-level positions, this is for candidates that have between three and five years of experience. Here, you're looking for someone that can work autonomously, perform investigations and coordinate with other teams. They need to have a good understanding of the incident response process and preferably have experience managing incident investigations.

1) Walk me through how you would coordinate an incident from start to finish?

    Here, you want to give them a scenario of a common incident that your company deals with or expects to deal with and see how they would go about handling that situation. Their answer should reflect most of the stages within the incident response lifecycle when it comes to doing analysis, containing the incident, and ultimately resolving the issue.

2) What is a SIEM?

    SIEM stands for Security Information and Event Management. A SIEM is responsible for collecting and analyzing security data that is collected from the different systems within a network to find abnormal behavior and potential cyberattacks. Some common technologies that feed data into a SIEM for analysis are firewalls, antivirus, applications, and network infrastructure devices.

3) What is the difference between HIDS and NIDS?

    **Host-Based Intrusion Detection System:** This is the type of detection system that monitors the system data and activity on an individual host.

    **Network-Based Intrusion Detection System:** This type of system operates at the network level and checks traffic from all the devices on the network to identify specific patterns of malicious behavior.

4) How do you harden a server?

This process is called system hardening and it's all about making a server as secure as possible. This is for the candidate to demonstrate their understanding of what causes hacks and how to stop them. Some of the points you want to look out for are: closing unnecessary ports, having firewall rules, changing default passwords, removing unnecessary services, applying all relevant security patches, enabling encryption, creating data backups, and set up system monitoring.

5) What is the difference between encoding, encryption, and hashing?

Encoding is a reversible transformation of data that is used to make data usable on different types of systems, it helps with availability. Encryption is a reversible type of data transformation that is considered secure because it requires the use of keys in order to decrypt the data, it protects confidentiality. Hashing is a one-way summary of data that cannot be reversed and is used to prove integrity.

6) Difference between processes, policy, and guidelines

A process is a set of actions taken to achieve a specific task. A policy is a set of rules that staff abide by as they carry out their day-to-day work, it is required to follow policy. Guidelines are a set of recommendations or best practices for completing a task, but they are not required. For mid-level positions, there may be situations where they are expected to update or create documentation for the team and it's important that they understand what the different types of documents are.

7) What is cross-site scripting (XSS)? And how to defend against it?

Cross-site scripting is a client-side code injection attack. This is when an attacker injects code into a legitimate web page or web application. Once someone visits that page, it will execute the code. To prevent it, the website or web application must sanitize the input. Sanitization means whenever you accept information from the user through a web form or other means, it must be checked for malicious code.

8) What is an automated incident response?

Automated incident response is about having processes and systemic ways to respond to potential cyber breaches. Rather than having to manually resolve incidents, automated response allows for machines to quickly take action. A common example of an automated response would be an antivirus software isolating a machine or a program on a machine that is displaying malicious behavior.

9) What is an advanced persistent threat and can you detect them?
An advanced persistent threat is a type of threat actor that gains unauthorized access to a computer network and remains undetected for an extended period. The goal here is typically to gather and exfiltrate information and secrets over a long period of time. As part of the incident response team, you may need to do threat hunting to check for these types of threats and you want people that understand what these threats are and how to detect them.

10) What are some of your professional achievements or major projects that you completed?
At this stage in their career, they should have some professional achievements or big projects that they have completed. Ask them about those projects and how their actions brought about positive results in those situations. This is designed to be an open-ended question that helps you learn more about their past experiences.

### Senior Level

For the purpose of this chapter, I'm considering any position that requires more than five years of experience as a senior-level position. In this position, they would be expected to oversee investigations and oversee other investigators to ensure that they are following the proper procedures.

1) What is a penetration test and what steps are usually taken in a penetration test?
They should be able to walk you through the different steps in your typical penetration test. This should include information gathering, scanning, exploitation, establishing a foothold and covering your footprints, etc. At this level, you want someone that understands in depth how an attacker thinks, what they are trying to achieve when they perform an attack and what their objectives are. It would also be a plus if the candidate has any offensive security certifications such as CEH, OWASP, etc.

2) Tell me about the hardest incident you ever had to manage?
This will give you a good sense of the level of incident experience that someone has had. If you're hiring a senior-level person you want

someone that has dealt with some pretty serious situations, this is someone that other people will look to for advice and direction on investigations so you want someone that really knows their stuff.

3) If you had a chance to build out your own CSIRT what would you do? This is an open-ended question that will expose the way that the candidate thinks about process and structure. As senior members of the team, they don't just add value based on what they can do but they add value based on how well they can make other people efficient. You want to see how this person can structure a team to be efficient because that will be a good indication of how they will influence your team if you decide to hire them.

4) What incident response team events have you participated in or overseen? One of the best ways to train your IR team is to have them engage in IR team simulations, CTFs, or competitions. It's a big plus to have someone that has participated in these events or overseen them that can lead the team in these types of activities. It's also a good sign that the candidate has some good training in the IR space and that they are capable of performing investigations in a short time and under pressure.

5) How do you deal with technical requests that you cannot figure out yourself? This question is to see how this person deals with troubleshooting. Anytime you work in tech you will inevitably run into situations where you don't know how something works or where the technology you are using is returning an unexpected error. As a senior member of the team, it's not good enough for them to simply give up and say that something doesn't work. You want to be confident that this person has strong troubleshooting skills and will be able to figure out the answer you need.

6) Have you ever done any threat hunting and if so please explain your process One of the advanced situations that you will run into is performing threat hunting activities on a regular basis. You never know when someone has breached your network without you knowing and is sitting on the network undetected. It's important that you have people

on your team who have the technical expertise to examine your network and find signs of these Advanced Persistent Threats.

7) What programming languages are good for automation?
Having someone that can automate IR processes through the use of computer scripts is very valuable. This allows one person to do the work of three to five people and that increases the productivity of the entire team. Some of the programming languages that you want to hire for include Python, PowerShell, and Bash scripting. These languages, especially Python, are most commonly used for automation in the security space.

8) What operating systems are you comfortable using?
As a security specialist, you can be required to work on many different types of operating systems; it's not enough for someone to only be comfortable working on windows machines. You want someone with experience with at least windows and Linux-based OSs. They should be able to navigate these file systems through the command line since not all machines will have a user interface for you to use.

9) How comfortable are you with computer forensics?
For an IR team to be effective, it needs to have an in-house computer forensics team, otherwise, you will have to consistently bring in third parties to do this work for you. Computer forensics is important for identifying how an attack happened and what actions were taken on the system and it's necessary to support any legal action if that is what the company decides to do.

10) How would you describe your leadership and communication style?
As a senior member of the team, you are looking for someone that will be able to help manage the team and ensure that everything is running smoothly. Therefore, it makes sense that you want someone with some leadership experience and someone who is comfortable giving instructions to other people on the team.

## REQUIRED SOFTWARE TOOLS

In addition to the generic security tools such as antiviruses, there are some specific security tools you need to effectively do incident response. Here are some of the security tools you should budget for when building out your incident response team:

**A Ticketing System:** The first thing you should invest in is a ticketing software that will allow you to create and manage records of the security incidents your team is working on. This will allow your team to be organized in tracking their incidents from start to finish, it will also allow you to keep a record of what was done and evidence of the actions that were taken, which will be important for auditing purposes.

**IDS/IPS:** In order to get information and alerts at the network level, it's important that your company have an IDS/IPS solution. This will allow the team to take action on any malicious activity that is occurring on the company network. Without this, the team will only be able to take action on alerts that are found at the machine level and they could potentially miss a lot of suspicious activity.

**Endpoint Security Tools:** This will be important for the team to monitor and get information on individual machines. This way the team can monitor changes at the file and process level throughout the organization. It's important that the team get alerts from both the network and machine levels in order to catch as many potential security incidents as possible.

**SIEM:** A SIEM is responsible for collecting and analyzing security data that is collected from the different systems within a network to find abnormal behavior and potential cyberattacks. Some common technologies that feed data into a SIEM for analysis are firewalls, antivirus, applications, and network infrastructure devices. SIEMs provide their analysis in two main ways:

- They create reports on incidents and events that can be used to determine what is occurring on your network.

- They can be set up to send alerts when a certain set of events take place, using predetermined rules. For example, you can set up a rule to send out an alert that if an admin account has more than five failed logins because it may indicate an attempted unauthorized login.

## RECAP

There are a lot of components to building an effective IR team. First, you want to take time to make sure that you have all of the core roles and responsibilities for the team filled. Next, you want to make sure that you have proper documentation to support the team. This is going to tell the team how they should act in certain situations and ensure that everyone is following the proper procedures. Lastly, you need to invest in the proper security software for the team. While the team will have to do manual searches through processes like threat hunting, the bulk majority of the team's investigations will be based on alerts raised through the company security software. If you don't have software or it's not properly configured, then the team will not be able to respond to potential malicious activities and the company will be at a much higher risk of a security breach.

# CHAPTER 8

# How to Pitch for a Quality Cybersecurity Budget

Cybersecurity is typically considered a cost center in most companies and therefore getting large budgets can be a problem. In order to do this, it's important to know how to quantify the ROI of cybersecurity so that you can persuade upper management to give you the budget you will need.

Getting funding for cybersecurity teams and projects can be a difficult task. Companies are in the business of making money and cybersecurity (generally) doesn't help with that. Therefore, you can face a lot of resistance when it comes to getting funding for software, hiring team members, etc. However, that doesn't mean you can't demonstrate and quantify the value of investing in your company's cybersecurity. Cybersecurity allows companies to save money that would otherwise be spent on fixing security reaches. Also, it helps to satisfy many mandatory regulatory or legal requirements that would otherwise cause lawsuits, fees, and potential suspension of business licenses. In this chapter, I will break down three approaches for pitching a budget to management that will help you make a convincing case for investing in cybersecurity.

## QUANTIFYING ROI

Return on Investment (ROI) is probably the single most important metric when it comes to business. It answers the question "For every dollar invested, what do I get back?". In profit-generating areas like sales, it's fairly

DOI: 10.1201/9781003264293-8

easy to calculate ROI because it's just Revenue − Cost = Profit. However, Cybersecurity is a cost center, meaning it doesn't generate profit for the business so it's a bit harder to calculate the ROI, but it's not impossible.

## FOUR AREAS OF ROI IN CYBERSECURITY

There are four primary ways that a cybersecurity initiative gives you an ROI:

- Reducing business risk

- Compliance with regulations or contractual agreements

- Reducing ongoing costs

- Meeting business objectives

**Reduction in Business Risk:** This is the primary means that an investment in Cybersecurity will pay back a business. Anytime the company suffers some type of security breach there is a cost associated with that. So by reducing the rate of occurrence for a specific type of incident, you save the company the money. For example, say Company A suffers 10 data breaches a year because of phishing emails that cost 10,000 to fix (10 × 10,000 = $100,000 per year). To fix this you implement a security control that costs you $20,000 but reduces the rate of occurrence by half, saving you $50,000 per year. Your payback in the first year alone will be (50,000 − 20,000) $30,000. This is one way a cybersecurity initiative can have a measurable ROI, but looking at the annual rate of occurrence, calculating the expected decrease in the rate of occurrence, and subtracting the amount of the control. Controls can be technical things like a firewall but it can also be hiring additional staff to do training or to respond and contain the situations as they occur.

### Risk-Reduction ROI

$$ROI = \frac{(\text{reduction in risk '\$'} - \text{cost of control})}{\text{cost of control}}$$

$$\text{Reduction in risk} = \text{annualized rate of occurrence} \times \text{expected monetary loss for a single event} \times \text{reduction in probability of risk occurrence with the implemented control}$$

**Compliance:** The next way Cybersecurity gives ROI is in the form of meeting mandatory compliance regulations. So there are two types of compliance regulations that apply in this situation – firstly, you have government or industry regulations. These will vary depending on your location and the type of industry the company operates in. Secondly, you have contractual obligations, so if you're a service provider for another company there may be clauses in the contract that say you have to have certain things in place from a security point of view. Failing to meet either of these compliance regulations can result in a lot of negative consequences such as fines, loss of clients, lawsuits, and, in severe cases, imprisonment.

**Reducing Ongoing Costs:** This means finding ways to optimize the current security or business processes so that it reduces overall costs. Some examples of this include reducing the required storage space or reducing time and effort through automation. Typically, this will never be the sole focus of a security project but it's a good additional reason.

**Meeting Business Objectives:** Security is usually a part of IT and they often have specific business objectives that they need to meet. One of these objectives that overlaps very heavily with security is availability. This includes things like recovery time objectives (RTO), recovery point objectives (RPOs), and having a certain amount of uptime. Any security project that is essential for or supports meeting business objectives is much more likely to get support and recognition from management.

## TIPS FOR COMMUNICATING ROI TO UPPER MANAGEMENT

**Give Good Estimates:** Use your best judgment, expertise, and software tools to estimate the risk mitigation for each investment. It doesn't need to be 100% accurate but you should be able to quantify the expected ROI for any risk mitigation project you invest in.

**Learn to Communicate in the Business Environment:** Security is not just a technical area, it's actually a part of finance, usually under a Chief Financial Officer (CFO). It's important to learn how to frame your ROI in terms of business objectives rather than just talking about "best practices" or "being more secure". It's better if you can talk about things like saving money, specific risk mitigations, compliance, RTOs and RPOs.

**Leverage Multiple ROI Arguments:** Rather than focusing on any one argument, combining multiple arguments to support one project/initiative will greatly increase the chances of success.

## HAVE ACCURATE ACCOUNTING FOR YOUR TEAM

The section "Four Areas of ROI in Cybersecurity" primarily focuses on how you can pitch for a cybersecurity initiative, like a new software tool by showing how it will benefit the company. When it comes to pitching for a budget for hiring staff, the conversation may be a little bit different. Upper management will want to know why we aren't able to perform well using your current team. It's the idea of "we've been working just fine up until now so why do I have to spend more money?". To combat this, there are a few different techniques you can use.

**Timesheets:** You should be able to speak to what each member of the team does on a monthly and weekly basis. You want to show that your current team is being used close to capacity and that it's not reasonable to expect them to produce beyond that. It's also important that you can demonstrate this for a long period of time. If you can only prove that your team has been working at capacity for the last 2–4 months then management can dismiss it by saying that it's simply a period of a lot of work and that we should wait to see if it will pass before you commit to hiring more people.

**Highlight the Consequences of Not Hiring:** You should understand the goals of your cybersecurity team and what objectives matter most to your manager. Therefore, one technique you can use is to highlight the consequences of not hiring someone and how that will negatively affect the team's overall goals. The important concept here is to understand that while the company as a whole has a bottom line, your manager and your team have specific goals that they need to hit and these goals are how you will be judged for promotions, raises, bonuses, etc. You need to show how not hiring will negatively affect your manager's chance to hit those goals; this will make it much more difficult for them to say no. Just be careful not to make them feel like you are boxing them into a corner or strong-arming them, just present them with the information, and let them make the decision.

**Highlight the Skill Sets That You Are Lacking:** Oftentimes when you are hiring for a cybersecurity team it's not simply a matter of getting more people. Many times you are hiring to make up for some type of skill deficiency. In situations like that, it's not a matter of showing how the team is being overworked as much as showing how not having someone with this skill prevents the team from effectively doing its job in the present or in the imminent future.

## USING INDUSTRY STATISTICS

If you're working for a company that has never had a serious data breach, then it may be hard to convince upper management of the money and time that can be wasted if a security incident isn't properly handled. One way to counter this is to provide industry statistics around the costs of improperly doing cybersecurity and this can help you to further justify why you need them to make an investment in the department. When you do this, you want to take it from reputable sources that management will be likely to trust rather than just from an online article or blog. To help with this, I've put together a list of 20 industry statistics that you may want to use if you ever have to put together a budget for cybersecurity and justify the money you are asking for:

1) On average, a security breach globally costs about $3.68 million, in Canada 6.75 million on average, and in the United States, that cost is $8.64 million.

   – IBM

2) Whenever there is a hack at a company that goes public, stock prices tend to take a dip; usually by about 7.27% on average.

   – COMPARITECH

3) If your company suffered a data breach due to what's deemed as inadequate security, you may face some compliance fees. GDPR as a prime example has collected a lot of money from companies due to non-compliance. In the first year alone, GDPR collected $63 million and Google was hit with a $57 million fine.

   – SECURITYMADESIMPLE

4) Cybersecurity Ventures estimates that ransomware costs will reach $265 billion by 2031.

5) A study by cybersecurity company BlueVoyant found that the supply chain is a major initial access point for cyber breaches. "A whopping 97% of firms have been impacted by a cybersecurity breach in their supply chain, and 93% admitted that they have suffered a direct cybersecurity breach because of weaknesses in their supply chain".

6) There's a cyberattack occurring every 39 seconds.

– UNIVERSITY OF NORTH GEORGIA

7) Cisco data estimates that distributed denial-of-service (DDOS) attacks will grow to 15.4 million by 2023, which will be more than double the 7.9 million in 2018.

8) DDOS attacks became more prevalent in 2020, with the NETSCOUT Threat Intelligence report seeing 4.83 million attacks in the first half of the year. That equates to 26,000 attacks per day and 18 per minute.

9) More than four-fifths of data breaches in 2020 (86%) were financially motivated, according to Verizon's 2020 Data Breach Investigations Report (DBIR).

10) For example, Verizon's 2020 DBIR found that 70% of breaches were caused by outsiders, 45% involved hacking, 86% were financially motivated, 17% involved some form of malware, and 22% featured phishing or social engineering.

11) Every minute, $2,900,000 is lost to cybercrime.

– FORBES

12) The average cost of downtime is 24 times higher than the average ransom amount.

– DATTO GLOBAL SURVEY

13) The average time to identify and contain a breach in 2020 was 280 days.

– CPOMAGAZINE.COM

14) 94% of all malware is delivered via email.

– VERIZON DATA BREACH INVESTIGATIONS
REPORT (DBIR) 2019

15) In 2019, 60% of breaches were due to exploited vulnerabilities for which a patch was available but not applied.

– HELPNETSECURITY.COM

16) Smaller organizations (1–250 employees) have the highest rate of being targeted by malicious emails at a rate of 1 in 323.

– VUMETRIC.COM

17) The average open source code library uses a version that is 2.5 years old and that leads to increased vulnerabilities.

– CONTRASTSECURITY.COM

18) According to the 2021 Imperva Bad Bot Report, **bad bot traffic** amounted to **25.6% of all website traffic in 2020,** up 6.2% from the previous year.

19) 86% of UK businesses experienced a phishing attack in 2020.

– *CYBER SECURITY BREACHES SURVEY*

20) There was an 80% increase in malware attacks on Mac computers in 2017.

– *CISCO*

## RECAP

For all areas of business, ROI is important, including Cybersecurity. The ROI of Cybersecurity often can't be calculated in terms of profit and loss but it can be shown through mitigation of risk, compliance, reduced cost, and the meeting of key business objectives. It's important to understand that more security isn't always better and you should not invest in any security initiative where the cost to secure an asset is greater than the value of potential damage to the asset. For example, don't spend $20,000 to stop a data hack that will only cost you $10,000.

# CHAPTER 9

# Why You Need Continuous Security Validation

The only way you can know if your company is currently secure is through security validation. You can do all of the theoretical planning that you want but if you don't actually put your systems to the test, then you won't ever know how they will hold up to stress. In cybersecurity, this is done through two different types of tests. First, you have vulnerability assessments. This is where someone will do an external scan of your systems to see what points of weakness exist. In this type of test, they simply document what the weaknesses are and send you a detailed list of all the weaknesses that they have found. However, they don't do any actual exploitation of those weaknesses in a vulnerability assessment so the amount of real-world feedback you get is limited. The second option is to do what is called a penetration test, which is where you have someone actively try to exploit these vulnerabilities and this is where you get a realistic picture of how secure or insecure your company's systems are. In this chapter, we're going to talk about why this is important and an easy way to implement this using bug bounty programs.

## WHY CONTINUOUS SECURITY VALIDATION IS IMPORTANT

For any modern-day business, having an online presence is mandatory. As you open up your business to the digital world, you become a potential target for hackers. As a business owner, you need to decide if you are

DOI: 10.1201/9781003264293-9

73

going to approach cybersecurity within your organization proactively or reactively. Having a reactive approach means that you wait until something goes wrong, such as a data breach or a cyberattack and then you take the steps required to fix it. Unfortunately, this approach is very common, especially for smaller companies that are more focused on profit-generating areas of business. Many companies subscribed to this type of thinking in the past but thankfully, more people are starting to understand that this approach is very costly. On average, hackers attempt a cyberattack every 39 seconds and the average cost of a data breach now exceeds $3.9 million per breach. Most businesses, especially smaller businesses, simply can't afford to be dealing with a data breach every year or even every two/three years. Roughly 60% of small- to medium-sized businesses that have a data breach go out of business within six months of the incident. To prevent this type of disaster, it's important that companies take a proactive approach to cybersecurity by investing in proper security validation. This means taking the steps to test and secure your business even if there are no visible signs of an impending cyberattack on your company. By making this initial investment in securing your company's infrastructure, you will significantly reduce the likelihood of a data breach in the future.

Having a proactive approach to cybersecurity comes in the form of conducting security assessments. Security assessments mean things like penetration testing, vulnerability assessments, red team engagements, and third-party evaluations. All of these methods are good in identifying where your weaknesses lie, the potential damage that can be caused by exploiting them, and what you need to do to fix them. Security assessments are an essential part of having a good cybersecurity program. However, they are not the ideal solution because they only provide a point in time assessment of your company. This simply means that they tell you how secure you are at the time the assessment is done. If you work in a large company, then you know that things are constantly changing, so a point in time assessment can become obsolete very quickly. For example, new technology is constantly being added/integrated, people are always leaving or joining the company, and there are new third-party vendors that are working with your business, which means new third-party dependencies. If you rely solely on a point in time assessment, you will get a snapshot of your company's security at the moment that assessment is done but this information can quickly become outdated as things change.

The solution to this issue is to use, what we call in the industry, continuous security validation. This way, you can be sure that even as your organization changes that your company remains secure. In order to do this effectively, companies should use popular threat modeling frameworks like MITRE to help them model their security testing after the exact attack vectors that cybercriminals are using today. This process is known as attack emulation and it's the process of using the same tools and techniques that attackers are using against companies that are similar to your business. This way, you can be sure that you are preparing for the exact type of attacks that you are likely to see in a real-world scenario.

## Emulation versus Simulation

As mentioned previously, an important aspect of continuous security validation is to have proper attack emulation, not just simulation. When you rely on simulating a cyberattack, this may lead to unrealistic results because the methods of attack are left up to the discretion of the tester, which may or may not mimic the attack techniques of hackers in real life. Often testers will use techniques that are too advanced and this results in security controls that are too strict to allow the business to run smoothly. On the other hand, the testers may use techniques that are not advanced enough and as a result, the security controls that are added are not strict enough to prevent real-world attacks.

You won't have this problem with emulation because this tries to use the exact tools and techniques of the attacker, which will lead to a more realistic and useful assessment. The goal of all your testing activities should be to recreate the attacks and situations that you would expect in a real-world attack. One common problem that many companies face is that they don't have the in-house expertise to perform these types of assessments themselves and therefore have to rely on outside consultants to do this for them. These outside consultants may be very skilled but they are usually very expensive and there's no guarantee that they will perform correctly either, they are still prone to human error and bias in the techniques that they choose to use. An alternative approach that I recommend that may be more cost-effective and consistent is to use a solution that can automate these assessments for you. One company that I have seen personally that offers this service is called rthreat; they offer a breach and attack emulation solution that can provide continuous assessments based on known, custom, and zero-day threats. This is just one company I'm aware of but you can find many companies that offer a similar solution. This way, rather than trying to keep up with the latest attack methods yourself, you can use a software solution that will keep track of these attack methods and test your organization against these attacks with minimal effort on your part on a consistent basis.

## HOW TO IMPLEMENT SECURITY VALIDATION USING BUG BOUNTY PROGRAMS

Another option for continuous validation is through the use of bug bounty programs. A Bug Bounty Program is an organized service where companies can have their websites or applications tested by freelance hackers. These freelancers look for vulnerabilities and give the hiring companies detailed instructions on how to fix those vulnerabilities in return for monetary compensation and points toward their ranking, depending on the platform that the program is running on. Bug bounties have been around for many years and are used by some of the biggest companies in the world such as Facebook, Google, Apple, and PayPal. They are the exact opposite of a bad concept in security known as "Security through obscurity"(STO), which means relying on the secrecy of a security engineering design or implementation as the main method of protecting that system. While STO can have some benefits, it's not something that you can expect to maintain for an entire website or application that is public-facing. If it's on the internet, its weaknesses will be found in time. Bug bounty programs take a proactive approach to this by inviting people to look at your system, find the vulnerabilities, and report the bugs to you before anyone with bad intentions has a chance to exploit them. Many companies run the program before going live to fix any outstanding security issues before releasing their product.

### Advantages

**You Get Multiple Opinions:** Bug bounties posted on big platforms can get tens or hundreds of researchers working on it at a time. This is good for you as an owner because you have more eyes looking for weaknesses, more people with different skill sets and techniques, and researchers with different levels of experience. This means they are more likely to find something interesting compared to hiring one consultant to perform the assessment for you.

**Relatively Cheap:** A good consultant can charge anything from $100–$500 an hour and some will charge even more than that! But, bug bounty programs can be significantly cheaper. Some bug bounty programs are free and only reward ranking points, which improves the researchers ranking on the hosting platform's website. This is common for non-profit organizations or charities that don't have big budgets and people won't mind helping them out because they know it's going to a good cause. If you're a bigger company and want to get the best you can pay something like $50–$5000 per bounty, depending on the type of vulnerability that they find. It's up to you how much you pay, but the more money you put in, the more effort people will put into hacking your platform.

**Scalable:** If you pay a company to do an assessment, you will usually have to agree to a price upfront, which means regardless of what is found and the severity of what is found you have to pay. With bug bounties this isn't the case, if a researcher doesn't report anything you don't pay them anything, you don't pay for duplicates of the same bug, and depending on how important the vulnerability is, you can decide how much you pay them. You directly pay for what you get. However, it's important you don't exploit this rule because if you get a reputation for not paying or underpaying, people will not want to invest their time in looking for bugs in your applications.

**You Make the Rules:** Another good feature of bug bounty programs is your ability to create the parameters of the tests. You're able to specify what areas of the application are off limits, how far you want them to take the test (stop when they find a vulnerability or try to exploit it and see how bad it really is), specify the dates of the test, rule out certain types of vulnerabilities and more. It offers you a great amount of customization. While you can do this in a traditional penetration test, the process is more tedious. First, is the procurement process where you find the company, get statements of work (SOWs), and negotiate price. Next, once you've decided on someone, you need to create legal contracts and have them signed. Then you must sign the tester's legal contracts that protect them in the event something goes wrong. Throughout these steps, there are revisions, edits, and negotiations that will take place. Bug bounty platforms simplify this process and eliminate that legal and procurement overhead.

Types of Bug Bounty Programs

**Public:** A public bug bounty program is one that is posted on a public platform and anyone that signs up on that platform can engage in the program. This is good if you want maximum feedback and exposure and you're not looking to hide anything on your application. It can also be a bit more cost-effective than a private bug bounty program because you're not bringing in specialists who expect to be compensated at a higher rate.

**Private:** A private bug bounty program is when you select specific researchers, usually who have very good reputations and you have vetted to engage in a bug bounty program. This will not be open to the public and will be invited only. The advantage here is that it will have a higher level of expertise and you are minimizing the amount of overall exposure your application or website has to the outside world. As mentioned above, STO isn't a be-all and end-all solution, but the fewer hackers that know about your product, the better, and this is what a private bug bounty will help you to do. However, because you're bringing in experts and all of the vetting that you need to do beforehand, you can expect these to be more expensive and time-consuming to organize than a public bug bounty program.

**Bugcrowd:** Bugcrowd was founded in 2011 and is one of the biggest crowdsourced security platforms. It has one of the largest and most comprehensive bug bounty programs and is a great place to consider posting your application or website for testing. Some notable companies that have used this platform include HP, Indeed, and Motorola.

**HackerOne:** This is another major player when it comes to bug bounties, HackerOne is arguably the biggest platform, in constant competition with Bugcrowd for the spot of number 1. Some of the big companies that have used HackerOne include Starbucks, Nintendo, PayPal, and Goldman Sachs.

Overall, bug bounty programs offer a great way to crowdsource security work. You can have the expertise of tens or hundreds of security researchers while only paying a fraction of the cost it would take to recruit them all individually. There are clear benefits to having so many people looking at your product. You can become aware of vulnerabilities long before someone with bad intentions gets a chance to use them and depending on the type of bug bounty program you choose you can limit the number of people that are aware of your application to a select group of researchers. These programs are not only beneficial to small companies but large companies such as Facebook have used bug bounty programs to improve their overall security and many companies would greatly benefit from implementing a similar approach [31].

## WHY YOU SHOULD STILL DO MANUAL TESTS

While point in time penetration tests do have some limitations, they are still very important. With the current level of AI and automation that we have, it's very difficult for software products to fully replicate the creativity and critical thinking that humans possess. Even if they try to emulate the same techniques and tactics, they will not be able to compare to a skilled professional hacker. It's in your best interest to have comprehensive penetration tests done by a professional at least once per year. Not only is this good for overall cybersecurity but many compliance regulations require that you have these tests done so in many cases it will not be optional. When doing these tests, you want to make sure that the professionals that are delivering this service are doing their due diligence to emulate the type of attacks that are most commonly used against companies with a similar profile to your own.

## RECAP

Continuous security validation and quality penetration tests are the only reliable ways to know if your company is resilient to cyberattacks. Often if you rely solely on industry best practices and implementing controls based on what you think the company needs, you are likely to overlook gaps and weaknesses in your system. This type of testing is designed to show you where you truly stand and it's well worth the investment to see how prepared you are for a cyberattack. Also, since many compliance regulations require that you do this type of testing anyway, it's a good idea to spend some time figuring out what the most cost-effective way of doing it will be.

# CHAPTER 10

# The Importance of Routine Simulations

The same way that routine penetration testing is important to ensure that your security controls are working, you need to do incident simulations to ensure that everyone within the organization knows what to do if a cyber-attack happens. This chapter will focus on the different types of simulations you can do, how often they should be done, and tips for doing them effectively.

S ECURITY INCIDENTS CAN HAPPEN at any time and like any emergency, you don't want to wait until the emergency to find out if your processes and your plan will work. It needs to be tested beforehand and regularly for you to be confident that it will work when you need it to. This may not be important for routine security incidents, but priority 1 and 2 incidents that have a high level of impact on the company need to be handled quickly and effectively. For example, think about something like a ransomware attack that can bring down an entire company's network overnight. A complete business outage like this can cost the company millions of dollars per day and it's critical that you can respond to things like this quickly. If the people responsible for fixing this haven't done dry runs they will be slow to act, they will act inefficiently and they are likely to make mistakes that can cost the company a lot of money. Here, we are going to discuss some of the different options for testing your company's resilience to different types of attacks. First, let's talk about some of the types of situations

DOI: 10.1201/9781003264293-10

that you want to simulate on a regular basis and then I'll get into the type of simulations that you can use.

## TYPES OF SITUATIONS YOU NEED TO PREPARE FOR

**Business Continuity and Disaster Recovery:** The purpose of Business Continuity (BC) is to maintain business operations following a disaster. BC and disaster recovery work together to bring an organization back to full operations. Usually, when a disaster happens your BC plan will allow your company to continue operations at a diminished capacity, so say 60% of your full capacity. While you are operating at 60%, you begin your disaster recovery, which is a plan that brings you back from your diminished capacity (60%) to your full 100%. 90% of small businesses that suffer a disaster and don't reopen within 5 days go out of business permanently within a year. A good business continuity plan outlines the procedures and instructions an organization should follow during different types of disasters. In this context, we are focusing specifically on recovering cyber-related events but the goal remains the same. You want to test that you will be able to remain operational during the attack and ultimately recover quickly and get back to full business operations. Now let's go over some of the specific cyberattacks you need to prepare for.

**Ransomware:** Ransomware is a type of malware that threatens to either block access to a victim's data or publish the victim's confidential information, unless they pay a ransom to the hacker. Ransomware is particularly dangerous for companies because it cripples a company's ability to operate by denying access to all of the information on the network through forced encryption. Many companies have information that is critical to their business operations and will choose to pay the ransom to get their information back. Ransomware is also one of the most profitable types of malware. In 2012, Symantec was able to access a command-and-control server used by a malware called CryptoDefense and estimated that attackers made $34,000 in a single day. They further estimated that they scammed over $394,000 in a single month. Symantec also made a conservative estimate that at least $5 million is extorted from victims via ransomware per year [32]. Due to its profitability, ransomware will continue to be around for a long time and your team needs to know how to handle these situations if they arise.

**DDOS:** DDOS stands for distributed denial of service, this is when someone tries to make a computer or console unable to respond or at least much slower to respond (lag). They do this by consistently sending traffic to that machine so that it gets overwhelmed and can't respond to legitimate traffic. While this doesn't pose any risk of creating a data breach it makes important business services like a website or web application unavailable to end users, which leads to a loss of business.

**Business Email Compromise:** This is when a business account has been taken over by an authorized user. This provides the user with access to company information and network resources, and gives them the means to send out phishing emails from an account that will look legitimate to everyone within the company. In order to prevent the attack from continuing to move within the network, it's important to have a smooth process for restricting this access and tracing back their steps to see what action was taken on the account.

**Zero-Day Vulnerabilities:** A zero day is a vulnerability that is either unknown to those who would have an interest in knowing of its existence or it is known but there is currently no patch/mitigation available for it. A zero day represents a big security vulnerability for the company and depending on the scope of the machines that it affects and whether or not it is being actively exploited then this needs to be a priority 1 security incident. Your time should do dry runs to ensure that they know who to contact and what needs to be done to get patches/mitigations pushed out across the company on a short notice.

**Insider Threat:** Insiders are threats to an organization that come from people within a company; such as employees, former employees, contractors, or business partners. According to IBM's 2015 Security Intelligence Index, 31.5% of attacks were by malicious insiders, 23.5% of attacks were by inadvertent insiders, and 95% involved someone inside the company making a mistake. Traditional security measures such as firewalls, antivirus, physical checkpoints, and others are designed to protect your company from external threats but are ineffective at protecting you from internal threat actors. In order to reduce this risk, you need to be prepared on how to quickly identify and neutralize insider threats.

**Phishing:** Phishing is one of the most popular types of cyberattacks and it's responsible for over 90% of malware delivery in a corporate environment [33]. While you can implement security features to scan attachments and block known phishing emails, it doesn't do you much good if people willingly choose to download files or click on URLs that are malicious. This is why you need to invest in security awareness training and phishing simulations that will allow you to measure how well prepared your employees are for a potential phishing attack.

## TYPES OF SECURITY TESTING/SIMULATIONS THAT YOU CAN DO

### Tabletop Exercise

A tabletop exercise is a discussion-based session that usually takes place in a conference room with upper management or executives. The purpose here is to look over the plan, use it in a few different theoretical scenarios, identify any gaps in the plan through brainstorming and ensure all business units that will be needed are represented in the plan. It doesn't take many resources and can be done routinely without causing a big burden.

### Structured Walk Through

In this type of exercise, each team member walks through their individual component of the plan in order to find any gaps. Usually, this is done with a specific type of situation in mind e.g. hurricane or earthquake.

### Simulation Testing

For a simulation, you gather all of the personnel that will be involved in the response plan and go through a simulation of an emergency and see how well the plan functions in that situation. These should be done at least once per year.

### Parallel Test

In this type of test, failover systems are tested to make sure that they can perform real business operations and support key processes and applications in the event of a disaster. Primary systems still carry the full production workload.

## Cutover Test

This takes the parallel test further and uses the failover systems to support the full production workload. You completely disconnect the primary systems. This type of test gives you as close as possible to a guarantee that in the event of a disaster, your failover systems will be able to support your entire business.

## LEVELS OF SECURITY TESTING

When you perform a test, you can test each system to a different level of depth. You want to ensure that your systems can be used to restore the production environment in case of an emergency. Here are some of the levels you may want to test your systems for:

### Data Verification

This level of testing aims to ensure that files have proper backups made but doesn't test that you can recover from those backups.

### Database Mounting

Database mounting tests that a database has basic functionalities such as being able to read the data.

### Single Machine Boot Verification

This tests that a single server can be rebooted after it has gone down. But doesn't prove that the server will still be functional and productive to the business.

### Runbook Testing

This includes multiple systems that work together to deliver a business service, such as a clustered database. This test serves to prove that a single business service can be restored.

### Recovery Assurance

This is the highest level of DR/BC testing and encompasses multiple machines, application testing, service level agreement (SLA) assessment, and doing diagnostics to explain why any rollback to system recovery failed.

## DISASTER RECOVERY TESTING BEST PRACTICES

### Test Regularly

The only way to know if your strategies, plans, and processes will work is to put them to the test. Despite this, only 23% of businesses never test their disaster recovery plan and about 33% test once or twice per year [34]. Most large companies test their plans quarterly and this is about the standard you should aim for.

### Use the Feedback from the Simulations

Once you have completed the simulation, be sure to take the information you have gathered and use it to drive your security program going forward. Make sure to get feedback from all of the key people in the organization that participated on what could be done to improve the process. This is your chance to improve and make things run as smoothly as possible before you have an actual emergency. According to Gartner, a technology research and consulting company, the average cost of IT downtime is $5600 per minute [35].

### Have Clear Goals

This refers to setting Recovery Point Objectives (RPO) and Recovery Time Objectives (RTO). RPO refers to how much data you are willing to lose before restoring your services and RTO refers to how much time can pass before services are restored, these together measure your ability to restore services on time and before too much data is lost. Additionally, some industry regulations such as health care require you to know and document your RTOs. About 65% of organizations fail their own Disaster Recovery Tests so it's important to focus on meeting these goals [36].

### Outsource if Necessary

Especially for a small company, you may want to use a DRaaS (Disaster Recovery as a Service) provider, they offer many services around disaster recovery including ongoing testing and 24/7 monitoring of DR solutions. Also, you may not need to outsource all of your recovery functions but consider outsourcing certain elements that you may not have in-house expertise for or bringing in outside consultants as needed.

**Have Cyber Insurance:** Cyber insurance is a specialty line of insurance that covers both businesses and individuals from internet-based risks. Cybersecurity attacks aren't covered in traditional insurance policies and therefore you need some extra cover for this type of risk. The different types of cyber insurance are as follows:

**Network Security:** This insures you against cyberattacks and hacks. This is the broadest and wide-ranging type of insurance. This is what most people will think of when they hear about cyber insurance.

**Theft and Fraud:** Covers destruction or loss of your data as a result of a criminal act or fraud. It also covers the illegal transfer of funds.

**Forensic Investigation:** Covers the Legal, Technical, and Forensic work necessary to determine whether a cyber incident has occurred, to assess the impact of an incident, or determine how to stop an ongoing cyber incident.

**Business Interruption:** This covers lost income and any business costs incurred due to a cyber event.

**Extortion:** This covers costs associated with investigating threats of cyberattacks against the policyholder's systems. It also covers payments to extortionists who threaten to take, delete, or disclose company information. A common example of this would be payouts to hackers following a ransomware attack.

**Reputation Insurance:** This provides protection against reputation attacks/cyber defamation. This is usually necessary if the hackers publish confidential information after a successful data breach.

**Computer Data Loss and Restoration:** This covers physical damage to computer-related assets and the retrieving and restoration of data, hardware, software, and other information lost as a result of a cyberattack.

**Information Privacy:** Covers liabilities from actual or alleged non-compliance to information privacy regulations. It also includes legal fees like a defense attorney or monetary settlement.

## RECAP

The only way to be sure that you are prepared for an emergency situation is to do proper testing and simulations. A simulation is simply a practice run of an event that will help you to see how well prepared you are for the real event. There are different levels of simulations. Some are more theory-based, such as a tabletop exercise or a structured walk through, while some are more practical such as a cutover test where you actually cross over to the backup systems and test your ability to maintain business operations during an actual emergency. It's equally important that you run tests for specific types of cyberattacks to ensure that your response teams know exactly what to do to defend against or recover from these types of attacks. The most important types of attacks to prepare for are ransomware, DDOS, business email compromise, insider threats, and zero-day vulnerabilities.

# CHAPTER 11

# The Six Steps to Preparing for a Cybersecurity Incident

This chapter focuses on the first step of the incident response lifecycle, the preparation phase. The preparation phase consists of six steps for making sure you have everything you need to prevent data breaches. While no method prevents all possible attacks, the large majority of cyberattacks come from a few main methods and these steps will show readers how to make sure their companies are resilient to those methods.

IN THIS CHAPTER AND Chapters 12 to 14, we are going to do a deep dive into how to effectively perform the different phases of incident response, using the NIST incident response lifecycle. NIST stands for National Institute of Standards and Technology and it's one of the most well-respected organizations in North America when it comes to standards and frameworks for technology. While this isn't the only framework you can use to model your Incident Response program, it's a solid option and most of the other reputable frameworks will be very similar to this one.

DOI: 10.1201/9781003264293-11

# INCIDENT RESPONSE LIFECYCLE

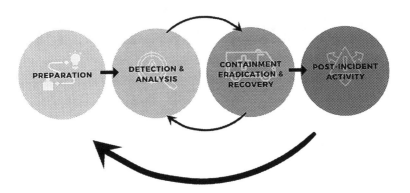

The first step is the preparation phase, according to NIST, this includes not only building out an incident response capability but it also includes making sure that systems are sufficiently secure to prevent incidents from happening. First, we're going to talk about how to build out the incident response capabilities.

## INCIDENT HANDLER COMMUNICATION

In this phase, NIST highlights the importance of having the right tools and resources for doing their job. They put a big emphasis on communication among the team, having the ability to notify incident handles quickly as well as the right people within the organization to support them. Here are some of the tool capabilities that you want to make sure are set up correctly:

Contact Information: You should contact information for all team members and important contacts within and outside the organization. This should include contacts such as law enforcement, consultants, tech support, and other incident response teams. This information may include phone numbers, email addresses, and instructions for verifying the contact's identity.

**On-Call Information:** Typically, you want to have 24/7 coverage of your organization and this usually requires having an on-call rotation. Therefore, you need to have a means of contacting the correct person on a rotation at any given time.

**Incident Reporting Mechanisms**: You need an efficient method of reporting when an incident happens to the appropriate person. Ideally, it will be a mixture of automated and manual processes. For example, in Amazon Web Services (AWS), you can configure the environment with cloudwatch (an event monitoring tool) and their SNS services (notification service) to have alerts sent directly to administrators. You should configure your security tools to send alerts directly to incident handlers when certain events occur. Second, for the manual aspect team managers should know who to report an incident to if they think a security issue has occurred or there is an issue that may lead to one. This information can be reported via email, text, or phone call, especially in time-sensitive situations. NIST also recommends that at least one mechanism should permit people to report incidents anonymously, this is particularly important if someone wants to report fraud/insider threat activity.

**Issue Tracking System:** As I mentioned earlier, this shows the importance of having a ticketing system that allows for tracking incident information related to security incidents. This means tracking what phase of the incident life cycle the incident is currently in, recording what actions are being taken and by whom, providing evidence of actions taken for later audits, and being able to share this information with authorized users in the company.

**Smartphones:** Smartphones are a good way to make sure that every member of the team can be reached quickly in case of an emergency. If possible, each member of the team should be provided with a work phone that is securely configured and the smartphone is to be carried by team members for off-hour support and onsite communications.

**Encryption Software:** Communications between members of the incident response team are confidential and can contain sensitive information. Encryption should be used for communications among team members, within the organization, and with external parties. This ensures that in a situation where the company has been compromised the communications will still be secure. For Federal Agencies, NIST notes that the software must use a FIPS-validated encryption algorithm.

**War Room:** A war room is a central room for communication and coordination during a crisis situation. This means that you should have a dedicated room for people to get together and work to resolve a crisis situation as it occurs.

**Secure Storage Facility:** As you do investigations, you need to have a place to store the evidence that you find, potentially for years to come. This information will be important for audit purposes, compliance, legal proceedings, and other business purposes. Best practices for secure storage include restricting access, storing the backups outside the company network, and having multiple copies.

## HARDWARE AND SOFTWARE ANALYSIS

**Digital Forensics Workstations and Backup Devices:** These are the devices that will be used to perform digital forensics activities. Some of the activities you need to be able to perform are creating disk images, preserving log files, and saving other important incident data.

**Packet Sniffers and Protocol Analyzers:** This is too used to capture and analyze network traffic. This can be used during threat hunting activities to find someone that is exfiltration data from the network, it can be used during an ongoing security incident to see what activities the hackers are performing on the network or it can be used for traditional network troubleshooting that may be causing a business outage.

**Removable Media:** Typically, this will be used to host programs that can be used to gather evidence from systems. It's generally impractical to install and uninstall the programs that you need for an investigation on every single workstation that you need. The better alternative is to install the program on a piece of removable media, that way it can be used on several machines.

**Evidence Gathering Accessories:** This list provided by NIST is geared toward ensuring that the chain of custody for evidence is solid and can be used to preserve evidence for legal actions. This includes hard-bound notebooks, digital cameras, audio recorders, chain of custody forms, evidence storage bags and tags, and evidence tape.

**Access to Clean Images:** You need to have access to clean images of OS and application installations so that in the event a machine is compromised or an application is corrupted you have a safe image that you can revert back to during the recovery phase of the investigation.

## HARDENING YOUR SYSTEMS FOR PREVENTING INCIDENTS

The second part of the preparation phase is to harden your environment so that there are as little vulnerabilities for hackers to exploit as possible. System hardening is the process of securing a computer system by reducing the amount of vulnerabilities that it has. When a computer is initially purchased and set up, its default configuration can contain many nonessential services and settings that may be used by hackers to get access to the system. System hardening is the process of removing or changing these default settings so that a computer can be as secure as possible before it is used in production.

System hardening is most important for machines that have a specific function such as a web server or a DNS server. These machines have very limited functionality and will be internet-facing, which means it's very important that they are configured to be as secure as possible. Performing hardening on systems with multiple purposes is possible, but you will be limited in the services you can restrict on a multipurpose machine because it will need to run many different types of services. In addition to system hardening, you have network hardening, which is where you attempt to make the network more secure by blocking unneeded traffic, having a secure network architecture, redundancy of important services, and other elements that make the network more secure overall. Here are some key tips that should be done in the preparation phase to limit the chance of a security incident occurring.

### System Hardening

**Remove Unnecessary Programs:** As mentioned earlier, every program is a potential entry point for an attacker. It's best to remove all programs that aren't necessary for the purpose of that machine. You should close any computer ports that are not needed. Ports are interfaces that allow a computer to connect to another device.

**Apply All Software Updates:** Outdated software is a very common means for an attacker to hack into a system. Outdated software is filled with security vulnerabilities that are disclosed publicly, which means hackers will usually be able to find out about them and exploit them very easily. Use service packs and keep all software up to date.

**Change Default or Hardcoded Passwords:** Keeping the default username and passwords make the job easy for attackers that are trying to gain access to user accounts. The default username and password of an OS is one of the first combinations an attacker will try, so it's important to change them before connecting to the internet.

**Disable Access to Firmware:** Firmware provides low-level access to a computer's hardware, simply meaning that they give you a significant amount of access to the hardware of the machine. This access should be disabled/restricted if it is not needed.

**Configure Security Features:** This means enabling antivirus/anti-malware software, configuring firewall rules, and enabling the secure version of the protocols you are using (ssh, sftp).

**Enable Encryption:** There should be up-to-date encryption algorithms used for data at rest and data in transit communications.

**System Monitoring:** If your organization uses any type of SIEM or other monitoring tools, this should be configured on the computer. This way you can monitor the system for any suspicious activity.

**Data Backups:** Proper backups should be enabled for all machines holding company information. This doesn't prevent a hack from occurring but it greatly minimizes the information lost in the event of something like ransomware. Also, it makes it easier to recover from a data breach if you have a recent data backup you can use to restore your systems.

**Use Hardening Templates from Reliable Sources:** Organizations like Microsoft and NIST have resources for helping you with securing your infrastructure. NIST has a guide to server hardening that goes over some of the best practices for securing a server, while Microsoft has a set of downloadable security baselines for their windows servers.

**Security Awareness Training for System Users:** Your users need to have a basic understanding of cybersecurity best practices for users. For example, you don't want them using their laptops for things that may result in them downloading viruses or being unaware of what a phishing email is, and that leads to their account getting hacked. There are multiple ways you can do this, many companies have required e-training courses that employees need to take whenever they start a position so that every employee should have a basic level of understanding in this area.

**Routine Risk Assessments:** You should have risk assessments done for your company periodically. This can tell you how your company's hardening templates compare to industry standards and if there needs to be any changes as new vulnerabilities and cyberattacks are developed each year.

## Network Hardening Tips

**Create Group Policies and Remove Unnecessary Accounts:** Group policies define what the members in each group have permission to do. Creating good group policies and deleting any unnecessary default accounts will help you to implement a least privilege model, where users only have access to do what is necessary for their job.

**Block All Unnecessary Traffic:** You should limit all inbound and outbound traffic to only the IP ranges necessary for business operation. For example, if an application is meant only to communicate within the network then all external communications should be blocked. Rather than doing this on a single machine, you can use things like firewall rules, network access control list, and group policies to apply this at scale in the organization.

**Network Architecture:** How you set up your network will have a big impact on how resistant you are to malware as well as how effectively malware will be able to spread on your network. Here are some of the elements you want to make sure you include in when making your network resistant to cyberattacks.

**Redundancy:** You want to make sure you never have a single point of failure for any critical business service. For example, if you are hosting a web application you should have multiple web servers that can handle a load of that application so that in the event of one server or set of servers going down that the business will still be able to operate. This may happen as a result of a DDOS attack, malware outbreak, code injection attack, etc. You should emulate this for any important business service that your company relies on and have redundancies built into the network architecture.

**Zero-Trust Model:** This is a security concept that states that an organization should not automatically trust anything inside its perimeter. Instead, it should verify everything before granting it access to anything. This means having continuous authentication even within the company network. Some people may assume that if something is inside the company network, it should be trusted. However, insider threats, advanced persistent threats, and legitimate accounts that have been compromised are all examples of things that sit inside the company perimeter but shouldn't be trusted and that is why it's important to implement a zero-trust model.

**Defense in Depth:** This is the idea that any important network resource should be protected by multiple layers of security. The same way you want redundancy for your network resources, you should not have a single point of failure when it comes to the security controls that you use to protect your network. Not only should you have redundant security controls but you should implement different types of controls that cover different aspects of security. Some common examples of this would the three following areas:

    i. **Physical Controls:** This includes all tangible/physical devices that are used to prevent or detect unauthorized access to company assets. This means things such as fences, surveillance cameras, guard dogs, and physical locks and doors.

    ii. **Technical Controls:** This includes hardware and software mechanisms that are used to protect assets from non-tangible threats. This includes things like encryption, firewalls, antivirus software, and intrusion detection systems (IDS).

    iii. **Administrative Controls:** This refers to the policies, procedures, and guidelines that outline company practices in accordance with security objectives. Some common examples of this will be employee hiring and termination procedures, equipment and internet usage, physical access to facilities, and separation of duties.

# CHAPTER 12

# How to Analyze a Potential Cybersecurity Incident

The next phase is to discuss how you should analyze a security incident. The first thing to do when you have a potential security incident is to analyze and answer questions such as: Is this a real incident? What's the scope? What's the potential impact?, and so on. This chapter will focus on what the correct questions to ask are and how this will be important for any investigations you have to do.

FOLLOWING THE PLANNING PHASE, the first step in handling a security incident is to perform an analysis. Analysis of a security incident is intended to understand the scope of the situation, its potential impact, and what needs to be done to contain and correct the incident. While some of this will be done manually the bulk of analysis should be done with the help of software to make the work much faster and more reliable. As an analyst, here are some of the things you should focus on during the analysis phase.

## IDENTIFYING IOCS

An Indicator of Compromise (IOC) is a forensic artifact that identifies a potentially malicious activity on a system or network. IOCs are important for both the prevention and detection of cyber threats. By inputting

DOI: 10.1201/9781003264293-12

IOCs of new cyber threats into software products, they can block any processes that match these IOCs and therefore detect the threat before it can get inside the network. IOCs that are used to detect an attack before it can compromise a network are also known as indicators of attack (IOA), they represent a proactive approach. On the reactive side, by scanning a network or machine looking for IOCs you can find a threat that may have infected the network already, then you are free to quarantine and delete that threat. IOCs are also heavily used in threat-hunting activities as one of the main things that professionals look for when doing manual searches, IOCs aren't just limited to being inputted into the company's software. During an investigation, you want to find as many IOCs as you can so that you can accurately determine if a cyberattack is underway and what the nature of the attack is. If done correctly you can even identify the type of malware down to its name and history and find the proper countermeasures using websites like virustotal.

Examples of Indicators of Compromise, Courtesy of Dark Reading [37]

- IP Addresses

- Domain Name

- Unusual Outbound Network Traffic

- Anomalies in Privileged User Account Activity

- Geographical Irregularities

- Log-In Red Flags

- Increases in Database Read Volume

- HTML Response Sizes

- Large Numbers of Requests for the Same File

- Mismatched Port-Application Traffic

- Suspicious Registry or System File Changes

- Unusual DNS Requests

- Unexpected Patching of Systems

- Mobile Device Profile Changes

- Bundles of Data in the Wrong Place

- Web Traffic with Inhuman Behavior

- Signs of DDOS Activity

- File Hashes

## UNDERSTAND THE SCOPE AND SEVERITY

Once you have determined whether or not the incident is legitimate you need to understand the scope of the incident. What is meant by the scope of the incident is how many systems and user accounts are being affected. This will help you determine what the severity of the situation is. In an organization, there are different rules and processes depending on how serious an incident is, so you need to have a means of classifying the incident. Typically, this is done using a system of P1–P4, with the "P" standing for priority. While this can vary between companies, the general requirements for determining severity will be the same across companies even if the categories that they use have a different name or number.

| Category | Description |
| --- | --- |
| P1 | Priority 1 is the highest level of a security incident. This is usually an emergency scenario where business operations have been halted or a critical system is failing. An example of this would be a ransomware attack that has downed the entire computer network. |
| P2 | In a priority 2 situation, this is where a major component of the client is affected but the business can still continue in some capacity. For example, if there is a DDOS attack that disables a company web server, this would be an example of a P2 incident because business can still continue despite this being a major setback. |
| P3 | Priority 3 incidents typically don't affect the core business but affect the operation of one or more people. For example, this could be an attempted brute force attack that has resulted in a few members of the company being locked out of their accounts and requiring a reset. |
| P4 | This issue is more of an inconvenience as opposed to a security incident that is causing a big impact. Typically, P4 incidents only affect one person and can be easily resolved. |

## UNDERSTAND WHO YOU NEED TO COMMUNICATE WITH

Most of the time, you're not going to be resolving these situations yourself, especially in a large company where there is a lot of segregation of duties. In these situations, you are going to need to coordinate with a lot of people to get something done. You want to identify this early on, so you know exactly who you need to talk to for the situation that you're dealing with. Who exactly you need to work with will depend on the type of cyberattack it is but here are a few you should always consider:

**Patch Management:** A ridiculous amount of security vulnerabilities can and will be solved by applying the proper security patches to the software. You want to know who is responsible for doing this and what the process is to get a patch pushed out quickly in your company.

**Legal:** The next team you want to have contacts for is the legal team (the lawyers). There are a lot of laws around user privacy, corporate laws, etc., that you may not be aware of so it's useful to have someone that you can consult with if there is a big security incident.

**Privacy:** If you have a dedicated privacy team in your company you should consult with them in any situation where a security incident has resulted in user data being leaked or stolen. They can help guide you on what you are required to do by law as well as your notification requirements to external bodies.

**Technical Investigators:** Sometimes you will require more technical expertise than what you yourself possess so it's good to have someone that you can call on to help you if a technical investigation needs to be done. A common example of this is if you need a computer forensics investigation done to see what a hacker may have done on a computer or to compile evidence that needs to be presented in court. You should have someone to call in these situations. It's great if you have this within your company but even if you don't have that expertise in-house, it's a good idea to have a third-party vendor that can provide you support in those situations.

## IDENTIFY NOTIFICATION REQUIREMENTS

Whenever a data breach occurs, you are required by law and regulatory bodies to notify affected parties. This includes regulatory bodies (depending on which industry you are in), regional privacy commissions, your affected customers, and third party vendors that may be affected due to a breach at your company. It's important to look into these different categories and ensure the right people are notified. Many times, there will be deadlines that you need to meet for notifying each party. It's important to know what those are so you don't miss the deadlines. You don't need to be an expert in this yourself, you should rely mostly on your legal team and privacy experts to identify this and handle the communications. But your responsibility will typically be to identify that the data breach has happened, notify them and give them the information that they need to accurately report on it.

## RECAP

Detection and analysis are all about accurately detecting and assessing a potential security incident. Your organization will get a lot of false positives from your security tools and it's in this phase that you need to examine that alert and determine if you have a legitimate security incident or not. If it's found that you have a legitimate security incident you need to begin your investigation and determine the scope of the situation and gather as much detailed information as you can. One of the most important of them will be gathering IOCs, which will allow you to find instances of the attack on your network and begin the containment process. The difficulty of your investigation and containment efforts will be affected by how well you perform your initial analysis of the situation.

# CHAPTER 13

# Steps to Containing a Cybersecurity Incident

This is the most important element to handling a security incident, which is how to contain it. Containment simply means ensuring that the situation can't spread to any other machines or user accounts. Effectively, this chapter will highlight how you can stop the bleeding when a security incident happens so that the damage to your business will be mitigated.

## ISOLATE ANY INFECTED ACCOUNTS AND MACHINES

This is the primary objective of the containment phase. This means preventing malware from spreading to any other systems or compromising any other accounts. Say for example someone in your company clicked on a link in a phishing email, this link downloaded malware on their computer and tricked them into giving up their login information for a company account. To contain a situation like this, you want to deactivate the account whose information was stolen and then isolate the infected machine by disconnecting it from the company network and the internet. This prevents the machine from spreading the malware to any other machines on the network, from sending emails to other employees, and keeps the malware from receiving instructions from the hacker via the internet.

Your first objective when it comes to containment is to stop the spread not to start removing the malware. It doesn't do much good to start removing the virus if it's spreading just as fast as you remove it. Many

DOI: 10.1201/9781003264293-13

pieces of malware, namely computer worms are designed to repeatedly duplicate themselves and spread to as many machines as possible. You will not be able to remove them faster than they can multiply if it is not contained. How you do this will vary depending on the situation, so we are going to go through some of the common ways to contain a cybersecurity incident.

1) **Disconnect Machines from the Network:** Whenever you are dealing with a malware outbreak, you need to disconnect machines from the network. This is done by removing the network cable (usually the blue cable) connected to the machine and will prevent the malware from being able to move from computer to computer. Be sure **not** to power off the machine. If you power off the machine you will destroy any forensic evidence that may be stored in the computer memory, which will make your investigation less effective. However, if you just remove the network cable, then you can prevent the infected computer(s) from being able to communicate with other machines and spreading malware without destroying that evidence.

2) **Isolate from Third-Party Networks:** If your company provides access to your internal network to other companies or has access to other companies' networks then you need to make sure that you isolate them in the event of a malware outbreak. In the event that you are breached, if malware from your network leaks into a business partner's network that can cause serious damage to them, it would lead to potential lawsuits and will have a negative impact on your business relationship, and vice versa if you are infected by malware from a business partner that spreads to your network. You want to be sure that in the event of a malware outbreak you are able to isolate from third-party networks quickly.

3) **Reset Account Passwords:** If you're dealing with a situation where there's no malware involved but an account has been compromised, then you use the same type of approach. If someone's email account has been hacked and it's being used maliciously you can contain that situation by disabling the account. This will prevent the hacker from being able to use that email account to steal company information or from sending phishing emails to other users in order to hack their accounts. Then, when you have a chance, you can reset the user's credentials so that they can go back to work.

4) **Block Outside IP Addresses:** In the event of an attack that is coming from outside of the network such as a DDOS attack or a brute force attack, your best means of containing this situation is to block the offending IP addresses. For external attacks like this blocking them is the only reliable way you can contain the situation.

## RECAP

The containment phase is all about stopping the bleeding. Ultimately, you want to contain an incident before it overwhelms company resources or causes serious damage. By containing an incident, you give yourself time to come up with a remediation plan and eventually resolve the situation. To properly contain a situation, you need to isolate all affected systems on the network; this way, malware can't continue to spread to different machines. Second, you want to make sure any infected machines are disconnected from the internet so that they are unable to communicate with the command and control server to receive instructions. Finally, any accounts that have been compromised should be disabled so that they can't be used by hackers to access company resources or impersonate any users.

# CHAPTER 14

# How to Eradicate and Recover from a Cybersecurity Incident

This chapter will focus on the final phase of handling a security incident which is how to get rid of the infection and ultimately recover from the cyberattack. This means returning to a normal state where all of the businesses' services and internal systems are functioning properly.

## ERADICATION PHASE

Eradication is the next step in this process, and this is simply where you get rid of any trace of attacker presence on the network. Oftentimes this means eliminating malware from infected machines, resetting account passwords, or any other action that will get rid of any attacker presence.

## HOW TO CLEAN MALWARE OFF OF A MACHINE

It can be difficult to properly get rid of malware off a machine. These are computer programs that are designed by people with a strong understanding of how computers work. Many malware programs are designed to redownload themselves, hide in folders, install themselves outside of the operating systems, infect other programs, etc. It can be very difficult to be sure that you have gotten rid of a virus but there are a few different methods that you can try with varying levels of certainty:

## PREREQUISITES

### Step 1: Disconnect from the Internet

Before you start working to remove malware from any machine, you need to make sure it's disconnected from your internal network and the internet. This way, there's no possibility that the malware will spread while you are working on it. For lesser malware like adware or low-severity security incidents, you may not need to take this step but for any malware that poses a serious risk to the organization, you need to make sure that you don't give it a chance to spread to other machines via your local network, and you want to disconnect it from the internet so that it can't receive instructions from the command-and-control server on the internet.

### Step 2: Make an Image of the Machine in Its Original State

Before you do any work on a machine that you're investigating you want to take an image (copy) of the machine in its original state. This is important for any type of forensic work that you do. Many things can go wrong during an investigation. For example, some malware are designed to destroy an operating system when computer forensic tools are used. You want to make sure you have a copy to work from in the event that something goes wrong.

### Step 3: Enter Safe Mode

When you load a machine in safe mode, you are loading it in its basic state using the default set of files and drivers. This way, you may be able to prevent the virus from running while you are trying to remove it. Safe mode is also a great way to troubleshoot machines because if the problem doesn't occur in safe mode, then you can confirm that it's something that was downloaded after the operating system was installed that is causing the problem.

### Step 4: Refrain from Logging into any Accounts

One of the main functions of malware is to steal user credentials as they are entered into login pages. While you are working on a machine that you think may have been infected with malware, avoid logging into any user accounts to minimize the risk of your credentials being stolen.

### Step 5: Clear Your Cache and Delete Temporary Files

Another good step is clear your web cache and delete any temporary files that have been downloaded as a result of the malware. This is a good practice that will help to remove elements of the malware from your machine before you go for a more thorough removal.

### Step 6: Malware Removal Techniques

**Complete Reimaging:** The best way to remove malware is to do what is called a reimage of the machine. To reimage a machine is simply the process of installing a new operating system on a machine. For example, if you have a Windows 10 laptop, to reimage it means that you completely wipe the hard drive of all files and items on that machine and install a new operating system. This way, everything that was on the infected machine will be removed and only a new set of files and programs will be on the laptop by the time that you are done. This way, you can be sure that nothing from the old operating system will be on the machine. The main reason people don't like to do this is because it removes everything from the old version of the laptop. So, if you want to keep anything from that machine you need to do a backup of it. Also, the amount of time that it takes to perform the reimage can be a deterrent to some people, but this is the most effective way of removing malware. As part of your incident response process, you should be sure to have "clean" images of your machines on hand for reimaging if you ever have a malware outbreak.

**Use Antivirus:** Most modern antiviruses have a feature that will allow you to quarantine and remove files that are suspected of being viruses. This is better than just deleting files manually but not as secure as doing a complete reimage. The reason being is that most antivirus solutions are pretty effective at detecting malware, but they can be fooled and circumvented. There are even some instances of malware that specialize in infecting antivirus solutions themselves to avoid detection so it's not 100% foolproof.

**Manual File Deletion:** This is the last possible malware technique and by far the less effective. Many people make the mistake of seeing a file that looks suspicious and simply deleting and uninstalling the program. Against most malware, this will not be sufficient because most malware is programmed to reinstall itself if it's just deleted by this method. At the bare minimum, you want to rely on your anti-malware solution to remove malware from your machines properly.

## RECOVERY PHASE

The recovery phase is all about getting back to a normal state of operation following a security incident. Unlike the other phases, there is not a particular set of steps that you can follow in order to achieve this so I've put together a checklist of things that you can look for to ensure that everything has been returned to normal following a security incident. This checklist will not be exhaustive, but it will give you a good idea of what you need to check for.

**Affected Systems Should Be Returned to the Network:** One of the first things that you do during a security incident is taking infected machines offline. Once you're confident that the malware has been removed and you have permission to do so, put the affected machines back on the network for use.

**User Account Credentials Reset:** If any user accounts were impacted during a data breach, you should be sure to have those credentials reset before re-enabling the account.

**Online Services Should Be Restored:** If any services were taken down as a result of the incident they should be restored starting with the most critical services.

**Take Steps to Ensure This Won't Happen Again:** Once you have restored business processes back to a normal state you should take steps to ensure that a similar incident can't happen again. This can be adding new security controls or simply making changes to business processes to prevent a mistake from being made in the future.

## RECAP

In this phase, you are focused on resolving the incident and removing any foothold that the hackers might have in your company. This includes doing things like deleting malware, disabling breached user accounts, and fixing whatever vulnerabilities allowed the hack to happen in the first place. For eradication to be effective, it's important to identify all affected hosts within the organization that need to be remediated and then apply the proper fix. For the recovery phase, you should be focused on returning all systems to normal operation. So any systems that were removed from production should be returned. Lastly, you should do an evaluation of anything that went wrong or that you weren't prepared for so you can make the adjustments for next time.

# CHAPTER 15

# What to Do If You Don't Have the Internal Expertise You Need

Many companies don't have a large internal cybersecurity staff and may not have the means required to handle a data breach by themselves. I'll go over the idea of outsourcing different elements of your cybersecurity program so that you have the coverage that you need to properly handle security incidents when they come up.

IN THIS CHAPTER, WE are going to discuss the benefit of outsourcing your cybersecurity operations. Many times your company may not have all of the necessary internal expertise needed to properly detect and resolve cybersecurity incidents and in this situation, it can be very beneficial to outsource your cybersecurity operations. Whenever you talk about outsourcing cybersecurity, you need to understand the term MSSP, which stands for managed security service provider. These are companies that provide outsourced monitoring and management of security devices and systems. Some common examples of this include managed firewalls, intrusion detection, and vulnerability scanning. The decision to outsource has its own pros and cons. Since every company is different, there isn't a single answer on whether or not you should outsource part of your operations but help you make that decision we've put together some of the common pros and cons of outsourcing cybersecurity operations.

## POTENTIAL BENEFITS OF OUTSOURCING CYBERSECURITY

1) **Lower Costs:** Typically, most managed service providers are specialists in a certain area and bring economies of scale, which means that they are doing this service at a large scale. This allows them to provide the capabilities that companies need at a lower price than what an in-house security team would cost the company to hire.

2) **Specialized Expertise:** MSSPs tend to have specialized talent around their service offering and this means that your company will get more specialized expertise by hiring an MSSP than you would by hiring your own staff.

3) **24/7 Year-Round Coverage:** For smaller companies, it can be difficult to get 24/7 coverage and if you do, it can be very costly having to pay employees to work overtime. With an MSSP you pay a fixed cost for reliable 24/7-year-round coverage which gives companies peace of mind.

4) **Reliability:** When you have an in-house security team, you are more vulnerable in the event that some of your key security staff leave the company. The smaller the team the more of a disadvantage you are in if someone leaves the company. MSSPs can handle turnover more easily and most of the time clients may not even notice when someone leaves their security team because they have so many people that can fill that role seamlessly. It also eliminates the overhead that the client HR team has to deal with because they won't need to spend time recruiting security personnel.

5) **Faster Detection and Response:** MSSPs tend to have larger data sets and typically better threat intelligence than what companies can do on their own, which allows them to have better insights into existing and emerging threats and how to detect and defend against them. Combine that with their 24/7 coverage and service level agreements (SLAs) which outline their required response times and you get good detection and response for cyber threats.

6) **More Experience:** MSSP security teams may be responsible for several organizations at a time and therefore will have exposure to handle more alerts and breaches than the typical in-house

organization will. As a result, they tend to have more relevant experience than most in-house teams and will be able to perform better, especially in higher-pressure situations than most in-house teams.

7) **Advanced Warnings:** Many MSSPs have good relationships with software vendors so when new zero days or threats emerge, they are usually the first ones to receive that information and can act on behalf of their clients quickly.

8) **Regulatory Compliance:** Since MSSPs deal with several clients across different regions, industries, and varying sizes, they usually have expertise in regulatory compliance across multiple areas. This can be a good value add-on for companies that may not have this expertise within their business.

## POTENTIAL CONS OF OUTSOURCING CYBERSECURITY

**Lack of Organizational Knowledge:** An MSSP may have an insufficient understanding of an organization's unique architecture, needs, and culture which can make it difficult for them to effectively do their job. While good documentation and meeting with internal stakeholders can help to minimize this risk, an MSSP will never have as in-depth an understanding of the company as the employees that work there every day.

**Worker Rotation:** If the MSSP doesn't prioritize keeping the same workers on contracting assignments, you may have a situation where you are working with a different group of people. This can make it difficult to get a consistent workflow because you are constantly dealing with a new person who may or may not be up to speed on your company's exact needs.

**Generic Security Approach:** Since MSSPs are responsible for multiple clients, they may try to use a generic approach that isn't properly customized to your organization's needs.

## HOW TO OUTSOURCE CYBERSECURITY EFFECTIVELY

**Evaluate Your Needs:** The first thing you need to do is take an inventory of what capabilities your company currently possesses. While many MSSPs may try to package several products together, you want to ensure that you are only outsourcing capabilities that your company doesn't already have. You don't want to have an overlap of skills unless your company is performing very poorly in that area.

**Examine the MSSP's Expertise:** There are two levels to this. First, you want to look at the MSSP overall and see how much experience they have in providing the services that you are looking for. You want to make sure that this closely matches your organization in terms of the type of businesses they deal with, the type of technology they will be supporting, etc. Second, you want to look at the security professionals that they will be monitoring your environment. You want to see their years of experience, qualifications and certifications, and past customer reviews, and, if possible, talk to them to see if they seem capable.

**Pay Attention to Your SLAs:** Your SLA is the most important document when it comes to outsourcing cybersecurity operations. This document will outline exactly what type of service you are entitled to as a client. It's important that you do an assessment of what type of response you need in any given situation and have it outlined in this document. This includes things like the type of coverage that you need, how long it should take them to respond to a cybersecurity incident, how long it should take them to notify relevant stakeholders, etc. You should also clearly outline what will happen if the vendor fails to meet the conditions of the SLA. Whether there is some type of refund for damages, legal liability, etc., this needs to be outlined within the SLA.

**Scalability:** You want to have flexibility in your services so that you aren't being charged for services that aren't being used. If you have services that you will need once in a while you want to have an agreement where you have the ability to get access to those services, but you are only charged if and when you invoke them. An example of this may be DDOS protection; this would only be needed during an actual DDOS attack.

## CYBERSECURITY OPERATIONS YOU SHOULD CONSIDER OUTSOURCING

**Vulnerability Management:** Every year, thousands of new vulnerabilities are identified in software products, each with different levels of severity. Some are simply bugs while others lead to major security breaches such as the WannaCry malware or the Solarwinds incident. Given the sheer number of vulnerabilities that a company is expected to stay informed on, you may want to consider outsourcing this to a company that has more resources to put toward managing these vulnerabilities. Also, there's the aspect of vulnerability assessments and penetration tests. These need to be done at certain intervals for regulatory purposes as well as for overall security awareness within the company. You can outsource one or both of these functions to an MSSP.

**Security Operations:** To have a truly effective cybersecurity program, you need to have 24/7 monitoring of your company's network. This is typically done through a security operations center (SOC). An SOC is a centralized unit within an organization that employs people, processes, and technology to monitor and improve an organization's security posture while responding to security incidents. Rather than trying to build out this entire operation yourself and upholding it, you may want to consider outsourcing the entire SOC operation.

**Recruiting:** Recruiting for technical roles can be difficult because it requires a niche skill set that can be difficult for HR people to effectively measure. One solution to this is to use recruiting firms that have a reputation for vetting cybersecurity talent. Typically, these companies only charge you once they place a candidate at your company, which can be a better alternative than having to pay for a full-time HR person. This is especially useful for smaller companies that don't have the budget for employees that aren't absolutely essential.

**Security Staff Training:** Unless you plan to outsource all elements of your cybersecurity program, you will have internal employees and the level of their training is going to be critical in how well they can perform their job. There's a good saying "You don't rise to the occasion, you fall to the level of your training". In an ever-evolving threat landscape, you need your security staff to stay up to date on the latest threats and best practices. Using vendors who specialize in security training is a great way to ensure that your in-house staff is as well prepared as possible for a cybersecurity incident.

**End User Training:** Now this type of training is for the everyday employee at your company. End users are typically one of the biggest security risks of a company. While technology can be configured to be secure by manipulating the settings, employees are a completely different story. Employees can be tricked by attackers using social engineering to perform many actions that may be harmful to the company and this needs to be addressed. Many companies opt to outsource end user training to companies that have specialized platforms and services for it. A common example of this is the mandatory e-training that many large companies have that you go through at the beginning of your job. Rather than having internal employees train end users, they simply have online courses provided by companies that end users must complete. For higher-level employees like C-suite executives that may be targeted more vigorously by attacks, they have specialized in-person training to ensure that they are educated on what to expect.

**Incident Response:** The function of incident response can be outsourced altogether. I already discussed above how you can outsource your security operations, which could include responding to security incidents on the day-to-day. When I say incident response here, I'm talking about priority 1 and higher security incidents. Some companies prefer to handle their daily operations themselves but keep large consulting companies like Deloitte, KPMG, etc., on retainer in the event that they are hit with a cyberattack that is beyond their current capabilities.

**Data Backup Storage:** The last thing on this list I want to mention is outsourcing the storage of your company's data backups. As a general rule, you don't want your data backups on the same network or physical space as your production data. The reason being that if your company gets hacked or suffers some type of physical damage like from a flood, then both your production data and the backups will be at risk. It's better to have your backups stored offsite at another location so that it is safe and be used to recover from one of these negative situations if it occurs. Unless your company has offsite facilities, it may be more cost-effective to use someone else's location rather than buying/renting your own. That's why you may want to consider outsourcing this service.

## RECAP

Outsourcing cybersecurity is a great way to get the specialty that you need without having to go through the process of recruiting a full team of professionals. The benefits of outsourcing are that you get better expertise, you can save money, 24/7 coverage, and less overhead because you don't have to manage the team yourself. However, you can't expect to have the same customization of services that you would if you had your security staff. Also, the MSSP will never have the same in-depth understanding of your company's infrastructure that an in-house team would have so they may overlook some aspects of your company. Whether or not outsourcing is right for your company is situational but it's definitely worth considering.

# CHAPTER 16

# How to Handle Third-Party Vendors That Have Suffered a Data Breach

In the event that one of your third-party vendors that you share client information with suffers a data breach, you will be required to take action. This chapter goes over what your responsibilities are in this situation and how you can manage these situations effectively.

A N OFTEN-OVERLOOKED ASPECT OF securing your business is how you deal with third-party vendors. As part of your business, you may need to share information, software, or access to your computer network with other businesses and this creates a potential security risk. Any information that you share with a third-party vendor is still your responsibility. If they have a data breach, you have a data breach and you will be responsible for notifying your customers and regulators, the same as if your company was the one that was hacked. Also, hackers can use the connections between different companies as a means to pivot from one company to another. A recent example of this is the Solarwinds incident. Solarwinds is a software company and once hackers were able to compromise Solarwinds, they put malware into their latest software update and sent it to all of their clients. Once the clients installed the new software update, they were infected with that same malware.

Another example of this is using business email compromise (BEC). If one of your third-party vendors gets hacked, the hacker can send you an email with malware that is disguised as a regular email attachment. Since you are already accustomed to getting emails from this company, most likely, you will open the email and download the attachment without being suspicious. These are just a couple of examples of how third parties can add risk to your business, which is why you want to do what you can to make sure you're protected from that risk of doing business. First, here are the three main categories of risks that come with using third-party services:

**Network Security:** If another company has access to your network in an insecure way this can lead to your company getting hacked. Sometimes, it may be necessary for companies to give their business partners access to their network to allow them to access certain resources remotely; however, this needs to be done correctly. Otherwise, any sort of malware outbreak from a partner company can result in that malware spreading to their business partners and infecting their networks.

**Regulatory:** This is where a third-party vendor that has your company's information is not compliant with one or more of the regulations that affect your company. You are ultimately responsible for ensuring that any third-party that you share information with is being handled in compliance with the applicable regulations. Not being compliant may result in fines or require you to suspend your business operations if it's a serious offense.

**Operational:** This would be any disruption to your company's operations where you're unable to provide products or services to your customers. A common example of this would be if you're using a cloud provider. If the server that's hosting your website goes down unexpectedly that means your customers will not be able to access your website and that will cost you business. If your company has a business model like Netflix that requires high uptime then this can be catastrophic to your business. Any dependency that your company has with their business partners that allows them to deliver their services is a potential operational risk.

## HOW YOU CAN MITIGATE YOUR THIRD-PARTY RISKS

**Identify All Your Third-Party Vendors and Their Contact Information:** You should keep a record of every vendor your company uses including their contact information, terms of service, and other relevant information. If a data breach happens with your company you need to be able to get in contact with them quickly, also you don't just want a general employee you want your point of contact because they will know if and how the data breach affects your company specifically.

**SLA:** In your service level agreement you should outline exactly what services you should be provided with. For example, it should guarantee a certain amount of uptime and in the event that this service is not delivered, it should outline what corrective action will be taken and any compensation that should be provided if they can't recover in a timely manner. You should have it in writing that your company should be notified in the event of a data breach and provide a dedicated mailbox for them to send the notification to.

**Use Industry Standard Vendor Assessments:** You can use assessment program's from established vendors like Microsoft or Adobe for assessing your vendor's risk level. These outline the security controls they assess for in every third-party vendor that stores or processes their company data. Here are some common examples of what you want to check for, provided by security boulevard [38]:

- Assertion of Security Practices: Review of security certification attestation reports (SOC 2 Type II, ISO 27001) and internal security policies and standards

- User Authentication: Password policies, access control processes, and support of multi-factor authentication

- Logging and Audit: Details about system/app/network logs and retention periods

- Data Center Security: Physical security controls in locations where company data is hosted

- Vulnerability and Patch Management: Cadence of external/ internal vulnerability assessments and pen tests as well as timelines for vulnerability remediations

- End-Point Protection: Policies that cover end-point security

- Data Encryption: Encryption of data in rest and transit

There are also vendor-neutral industry standards that you can use to in assessing your vendor's risk management, here are some of the popular ones:

- SOC 2

- ISO 27001

- Consensus Assessment Initiative Questionnaire

- NIST Risk Management Framework 2.0

- NIST 800-171

- VSA Questionnaire

- CIS Critical Security Controls

**Give as Little Information as Possible:** You want to make sure you only give information that is absolutely necessary for the vendor to do their job. You should be able to give a business reason for every piece of information you give to your vendors. Additionally, if possible you should break the information up so that it can't be used to identify an individual. For example, something like a social security number by itself isn't very useful, but if you have a person's first name and last name along with the social security number then it becomes much more useful for fraud. So wherever possible break up the information so that it can't be used to harm anyone. This process is called data anonymization and it's the process of protecting private and sensitive information by erasing or encrypting identifiers that connect an individual to stored data.

**Monitor the News for Your Vendors:** As mentioned earlier if your vendors suffer a data breach you are ultimately responsible as the owner of that information. Therefore, it's important that you keep tabs on your vendors to see if they are affected by any data breaches so that you can be on time with your notification requirements and take all of the required steps to protect your consumer's information.

**Get Involved if a Data Breach Occurs:** If your vendor does suffer a data breach you have two main objectives. Firstly, you want to know if this directly affects the security of your company. For example, if they have a malware outbreak and they have access to your company's network, you need to consider if it may have spread to your company as well. Also, if someone's email account was hacked within that vendor, then you need to see if they sent any phishing emails to your company because if someone clicked on the link or downloaded any attachment, your company may be affected. Secondly, you should get a statement from the vendor confirming if any of your company's information was leaked. This statement is important for proving you did your due diligence in investigating the incident.

**Have Good Onboarding and Offboarding Processes:** You want to have a standard onboarding process for new vendors. During onboarding, you want to make sure they understand your information security standards/policies, any compliance requirements that you have, and have agreed to adhere to those standards. Once your business relationship has ended it's important that you off-board your vendors, this means having them delete all of your company's information from their systems and getting written confirmation that they have done so.

**Use Security Ratings:** You can use security ratings to monitor how secure your vendors and their vendors are in real time. Tools such as BitSight use open source intelligence to evaluate your vendors. They can monitor several vendors at a time and can save you a lot of time from having to do that research yourself. They can also be set up to alert you if your vendors are mentioned in the news for having a data breach. However, most of these tools are not free and can be quite expensive.

## RECAP

Third parties represent a unique risk for businesses, any company that has access to your company's network or holds company data for processing or any other type of business service is a potential risk. No matter who you share your data with, your company will also be responsible for ensuring that the information is properly protected and handled according to the proper data privacy laws. The way you do this is through proper onboarding and offboarding of your vendors. You want to outline your expectations to them when it comes to protecting company information and upholding data privacy. Be sure to have this written down as part of your contracts and have the vendor agree to it. You can also reduce your overall risk by simply making sure that you are only sharing information that is absolutely necessary for business purposes and anonymizing the information wherever possible. If the information cannot be linked back to an individual, then even if it gets leaked, it's not considered a breach of privacy because it's not a personally identifiable information. Through the business relationship, you want to make sure that you stay informed of any data breaches that occur with your vendors or their immediate vendors to be aware of any potential leak of your company's information. If any of your company's information is leaked, you need to fulfill all of your obligations when it comes to notifying affected parties and doing what you can to remediate the situation. Lastly, you want to have a good offboarding process. This means ensuring that all company information is deleted from the vendor's network once the business relationship has ended. Once there is no longer any business need for the company to have the information, it should be deleted; even if the companies still have a business relationship, once the data that they are holding is no longer needed, then it should be deleted as soon as possible.

# CHAPTER 17

# How to Remove Data Leaks Once They Are on the Internet

For certain types of incidents, your company's information may be posted online such as client information on a website or company secrets accidentally uploaded to GitHub. Another situation is someone using domains that are associated with your business name. In situations where you have information on other platforms that are negatively affecting you, you need to understand the proper methods for getting them removed or remediated.

ONE OF THE THINGS that will happen when your company gets hacked is that you will have to deal with data leaks. This can be malicious such as when someone hacks into your company and posts your information online because you fail to pay them a ransom or for some other reason. It can also be non-malicious such as when a developer accidentally makes a GitHub commit that contains sensitive information such as company usernames, passwords, customer information, access keys, etc. This can cause a lot of issues for your business because once something is on the internet, it can be extremely difficult to get it taken down and almost impossible to get the footprint completely removed. However, there are some things you can do if you find yourself in this situation, as these situations have become more and more common. Companies and governing bodies have come up with processes to help businesses that need to get their information removed from websites and forums. In this chapter, we are going to go over some of the common situations that you are likely to encounter and what you can do to resolve them.

## HOW TO REMOVE DATA LEAKS ON GITHUB

While GitHub is a great place for sharing code, it's also a common place for people to accidentally leak company secrets. The problem is when developers post code to GitHub, they can unintentionally post company information that is hidden within that code, including but not limited to IP addresses, domain names, passwords, usernames, emails, and access keys. The first step in getting these data leaks contained is to detect them. However, in any company of a size that has tens or hundreds of developers and consistent turnover, it's impractical to think that you can simply manually check each developer's GitHub repos to make sure that they haven't posted anything that they shouldn't have. The best way to detect when this occurs is through the use of automated software tools, known as secrets detection tools. Here are some popular examples you can use:

### Truffle Hog

TruffleHog is a security tool that can detect company secrets across multiple platforms, including GitHub, GitLab, AWS S3, JIRA, Confluence, Slack, and more. Not only that but unlike other tools that do point in time assessments, TruffleHog runs constantly in the background scanning for company secrets across multiple platforms, and will send you an alert whenever a match is found. Another useful feature is that it has automatic updates so that it's always up to date with the best regular expressions for secrets detection.

### GitSecrets

GitSecrets is an open source command line tool that you can use to proactively prevent company secrets from being committed to GitHub. What GitSecrets does is that it scans developer commits and merges, if anything in those actions matches a regular expression pattern then the commit will be rejected before it can get to GitHub.

### GitHub Secret Scanning

GitHub has its own secret scanning solution that can be used to find API Keys and tokens stored in any public GitHub repository. Scanning private repositories is possible but will require an Advanced Security License. You can scan for other types of secrets like passwords, emails, etc., by creating your own custom regular expressions formulas.

### GitLeaks

Gitleaks is an open source command line static analysis tool. This tool is used to find hard-coded secrets in both private and public repositories using regular expressions and entropy string coding. It also has the capability to export reports of its findings in either JSON, SARIF, or CSV formats. GitLeaks can also scan commit history and hook into your CI/CD pipeline.

### SpectralOps

This tool is a comprehensive commercial solution for secret scanning and detection through the entire build process. Unlike many other tools on this list, it comes with an intuitive user interface and its AI and machine learning algorithms are constantly being updated by the spectral team to allow for better secrets detection.

### GitGuardian

GitGuardian is another commercial solution that does secret detection and remediation on both public and internal repositories. They are a full-fledged application rather than just a command line tool, which makes it much easier to use and they have even done a side-by-side comparison with highly popular tools like TruffleHog so you can see how GitGuardian compares to other popular tools. They also give you the option to demo their product so you can see how you like it before you commit to them.

## HOW TO GET A GITHUB DATA LEAK REMOVED

Once you have found an instance where some of your company information has been leaked on GitHub, you have two primary options for removal.

1) **Contacting the User:** This should be your first option because not only is it typically quicker but it can give you some additional information about what was leaked. If you look at a GitHub profile page you can usually find a name and maybe even contact information for the user (who most often is an employee or former employee).

Your best bet is to simply ask them to remove the repo because of security reasons and many times, they will happily do so. The second benefit of this is that by contacting the user, you can get an understanding of what was leaked, how it could be used, and if the information is still relevant. For example, if you use one of the tools mentioned above and get a hit that a GitHub repo has an access key in it. While you know that an access key provides access to company services and shouldn't be open to the public you may not know what service this key is for and if it's still active. By communicating with the user, you can get a better idea of what the risk is to your business and what you need to do to remediate it. If the key is still active, just deleting it is not enough because someone may have already seen it and copied it down, you would need to change that access key to prevent someone from being able to use it in addition to removing it from GitHub.

2) **Submit a Request with GitHub:** In the event that you can't contact a user or they are being unresponsive, you can submit a request with GitHub to have the repository taken down. You can do this by looking for "Submit a Private Information Removal Request". Here, you can outline the GitHub repo that you need removed and give the justification for why it should be removed. Once you have done that it should take GitHub between 24 and 72 hours to remove the repository. I would advise that you make a copy of the repository before doing this so that you can keep track of what was leaked and do your own investigation to ensure that the information cannot be used by an attacker to gain access to the company.

## HOW TO PREVENT DATA LEAKS ON GITHUB

### Educate Your Developers

The best thing you can do to prevent this is to educate your developers on the risks that this poses to the company and how they can tell if the code they want to post is suitable for a public repo. They need to be educated on how things like IP addresses, access keys, usernames, passwords, etc., can be used by hackers and how they can be held liable if they post this information and it's used against the company. They have the option to not post the information at all or keep it in a private repository if it needs to be shared with other members of the team.

### Use Fake Data

As a general best practice, developers should not be using real customer data when working on new code. Production data has certain privacy requirements and it's best to simply use fake data that has the same structure as the production data. If you need a physical address to use in the code to see if it will work, you don't need a real address. You can use a fake address that has the same structure as a real address and it should be just as good for testing purposes. If this test data is leaked on GitHub, then it's not a big deal and poses no risk to the company.

### Use a Monitoring Service or Tool

Lastly, you should have a means of monitoring GitHub for any leaked secrets. While you can do all of the preventative controls that you want, there is a high probability that some things will still get leaked to GitHub and you need a way of catching that. One way you can do it is to have a bug bounty program where you pay people for any company secrets that they find. Alternatively, you can use one of the tools or services mentioned in the previous section to periodically scan GitHub for any company secrets that may have been leaked. Either way the important thing is that you have a means of scanning GitHub periodically for any leaked information.

## WHAT HAPPENS IF SOMEONE POSTS YOUR COMPANY'S DATA ONLINE?

Another thing you have to worry about is someone stealing your company's information and posting it online. This can happen for many reasons. Firstly, when hackers steal your information, sometimes, they will threaten you with leaking that information if you don't pay them a certain amount of money. Secondly, sometimes, hackers will sell the stolen information to other people in order to make a profit. Thirdly, some people will simply post information about your company (whether true or not) in an attempt to defame the company, give other people the means to hack you, or damage the business's reputation. In any event, you want to know what your options are for having this information removed if you ever come across it.

### Contact the Owner of the Forum/Website

This one is the most obvious but it's the easiest and definitely the first thing you should try. If someone is posting confidential information on a popular forum like Reddit for example, the first thing you can try is to report it and contact an admin that can get the comment removed and the person banned. However, this can only be used when the data is put on a legitimate platform.

### Submit a Request with Google

If you ever have a situation where you have company or personal information posted on a website and you are unable to get the owner to take the information down you can submit a request with Google to have the website removed from search results. While this doesn't control the content on the website, it can prevent the website from appearing on Google search results which will reduce the number of people that will find the site and therefore reduce the overall exposure of that information to the public. Just be sure to have a detailed explanation as to why the information should be removed.

### Report the Website to Law Enforcement or the Web Hosting Provider

If you actually want to get the website shut down and removed from the internet completely without the help of the owner, then you are going to need to report the website to law enforcement or the web-hosting provider directly. The best way to do this is to start by reporting it to your local law enforcement agency and then following it up by filing a complaint online with the Internet Crime Complaint Center (ICCC). They are affiliated with the FBI and work to resolve incidents of cybercrime. If what they have posted is in fact against the law, then these agencies should be able to help you get the website taken down. However, if what is posted is simply something you do not like and doesn't violate any laws, then there's not much they can do to help you.

## HOW TO PREVENT SOMEONE FROM POSTING YOUR DATA ONLINE

### Protect Your Data

The first thing you should do to prevent your data from being posted online is making sure that it is properly protected within the business. You should have defense in depth. Defense in depth is the idea that any important network resource should be protected by multiple layers of security. You should not have a single point of failure when it comes to the security controls that you use. Not only that but it requires that you implement a variety of different controls that cover different aspects of security. You can think of each of these aspects as layers and a good defense in-depth strategy will have controls that cover each area of security.

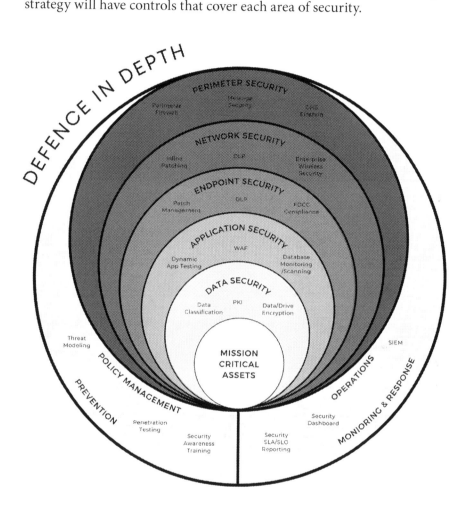

## Anonymize Client Information

The next thing you can do to prevent a data leak is to anonymize any personal information that you hold in your business. When information is leaked to the public, it can only be considered personal information if it can be connected to an individual person. If you take steps to disconnect information from the person it belongs to, then that information becomes much less useful and hackers will be less likely to target it because it doesn't hold any value to them. Even if they do steal the information and post it, the information will be harmless and it wouldn't even constitute a data breach.

## WHAT HAPPENS IF SOMEONE STEALS MY DOMAIN?

The last thing on this list that you may come across when it comes to company information being posted online is when someone tries to steal your domain. While this may not be a leak of confidential company information, what hackers will usually do is they will take information from your company website, and the company brand, and they will use that information to create a fake website or webpage and give it a domain similar to your company's true domain. For example, if they are trying to impersonate a company like Facebook, they may use a common typo domain like Faceboook or something to that effect. With thousands of people trying to type in that URL, it's only a matter of time before some make that mistake and be directed to the fake website. This is an example of cybersquatting, which is the registering or use of an internet domain with bad intent to profit from the goodwill of a trademark belonging to someone else. If you find someone doing this, you have the right and ability to get that domain taken down.

All top-level domains based on copyright or trademarked words/phrases are protected under what's called the Uniform Domain-Name Resolution Policy (UDRP). This means that you, as the owner of the copyright or trademark, have claims on domains registered in bad faith related to your intellectual property. Bad faith includes but is not limited to disrupting a competitor, profiting from an assumed connection between the material and the owner of the domain, or attempting to block the rightful owner from registering the name themselves.

## WHAT TO DO ABOUT A SQUATTED DOMAIN

If you find a domain that you believe is registered in bad faith, you should begin by either contacting the domain owner or filing a UDRP claim or court proceeding. When filing this claim, you should choose an Internet Corporation for Assigned Names and Numbers (ICANN) approved provider to oversee the proceedings. If you've never heard of it before, ICANN is a not-for-profit partnership dedicated to keeping the internet secure, stable, and interoperable. They specialize in coordinating the internet's naming system, which is why this falls under their domain. You will need to provide evidence of the trademark or copyright ownership as part of the dispute.

## HOW TO PREVENT DOMAIN SQUATTING

The best way to avoid this situation is to prevent it from happening in the first place; here are some of the things you can do to prevent someone from registering your domain.

### Register the Domain Before You Need It

You want to buy your domain as soon as you are certain of what you are calling your business or copyright material. Domain squatters often buy recently searched domains in the hopes of selling them to the original searcher so you want to avoid doing a lot of research and not buying the domain. Domains are relatively cheap and it will save you a lot of time and money in the long run just to buy them upfront.

### Register Similar Names

When people are entering their names, they may have misspellings or use different extensions based on where they live or what they are used to. You want to buy a domain with multiple extensions such as .com, .ca, .org, etc., so that no one else can register these domains. Also, research common misspellings of your domain and consider registering them as well.

### Purchase Domain Ownership Protection

This protection helps to ensure that you retain the registration of a domain regardless of expiration dates or attempts to transfer. This is important because if you have a popular domain, people will be constantly trying to buy that domain and if your credit card declines or you forget to renew your domain ownership for even a few hours, you can end up losing your domain. Buying domain ownership protection helps to mitigate this risk.

### Register a Trademark

You maintain your legal right to a domain by having a registered trademark, not just claiming the domain. Therefore, you want to make sure that you have a registered trademark with the patent office in your area.

### Be the Owner on Record

If you are a business owner and you have someone else register the domain on your behalf, make sure they do it in your name and not their own. Otherwise, if you have a dispute later on, they may be able to take your domain name if they originally registered it in their name.

## RECAP

It's common for company data to be leaked onto the internet. Even if your company doesn't have a formal data breach or hack, just through employee negligence or day-to-day transactions, company data can be leaked to the web. This information can pose a serious security risk, especially if it's information that has been hard-coded into company code bases and posted online on platforms like GitHub. It's important that your company has a means of scanning the web for these data leaks and taking action to get them removed as soon as possible. Similarly, you can run into situations where company information is posted on online forums or you may have people that use your public information to create duplicates of your company websites. In that situation, you need to contact either the website owner, ICANN provider, and/or law enforcement to have that information removed.

# CHAPTER 18

# How to Address the Public During a Data Breach

As part of your overall incident handling process, you should keep the public informed of what the situation is and how you are handling it. This way people are more comfortable knowing that the situation is being handled and that they have support. Also, you don't want people speculating on the situation, feeling that you are not doing your due diligence or even filing lawsuits because they find out through a third party about a data breach involving their data. This chapter will teach readers how to control the narrative around their data breach.

O NE OF THE NON-TECHNICAL issues businesses face during a data breach is media obligations. There are many regulatory bodies such as HIPAA or GDPR that require you to inform your customers and business partners when a cybersecurity incident occurs. However, this can be difficult because many businesses are worried about the effect that this can have on their business's reputation, potential loss of business and overall seeming incompetent in the media. On average, 29% of businesses that suffer a data breach end up losing revenue and of that 29%, 38% experienced a loss of revenue of at least 20% or more [39]. Being able to properly handle media obligations, notification requirements, and framing things the correct way is an important thing to understand when you're going through a security crisis. Here are some key tips to ensure that you minimize the negative impact on the media when you have a security breach that you are required to report on:

## UNDERSTAND YOUR REPORTING OBLIGATIONS

Depending on your Company's Industry and area you will have specific requirements on who you need to notify when a data breach occurs. There are four things you need to be aware of.

1) **Who Needs to Be Notified:** This will usually include a regulatory authority for your industry, impacted customers, third-party vendors, and anyone else whose information has been impacted or who may be at risk as a result of the data breach.

2) **Be Aware of Your Timeline:** There are almost always time restrictions that mandate when you need to inform each group. In order to be compliant with the law, you need to be aware of this.

3) **Know the Medium You Should Use:** According to the laws that govern your business, you may be required to use certain communication mediums such as email, mail, or phone call. It's important to know which options are available to you before sending out the notice.

4) **Know the Areas You Do Business In:** The laws governing your breach notification requirements are not just based on where your business is operating. It is also based on where your customers live. For example, if your business is based in California but you collect consumer information in Florida, you are subject to the laws that govern consumer information in Florida.

Fortunately, many different companies have online databases that outline notification requirements in different areas. In order to make sure you are fulfilling your requirements, I would suggest using multiple sources and preferably state/government sources to identify your requirements.

## HOW TO DEAL WITH THE MEDIA

Once you have identified your notification requirements and the groups of people that need to be informed, you need to figure out the best way to approach it.

**Talk about What You Know:** Keep in mind that once you put information out there, it is there forever. Going back on what you've said in the past can make you look incompetent and will make people doubt what you have to say going forward. Avoid the temptation to say things like "there was no data leakage" unless absolutely sure; instead, saying something like "we have found no evidence of data leakage and we will continue to give out updates as new information becomes available" gives the same information but gives you more wiggle room if you find out later on that people's information was leaked. Try to avoid using absolute statements, especially early on.

**Make Yourself Easy to Find:** Once you have announced a data breach, many consumers and businesses will be looking for information on how this situation affects them. It's a good idea to have a place where new updates on the situation are posted so that this information is easily accessible. Usually, this is on a company's blog page, where updates are constantly added as new information comes in. You can also provide a number to a company representative for people to contact if they have specific questions, but the point here is to make sure you are easy to contact.

**If Applicable, Reference Other Companies:** If the attack that led to your data breach has affected other companies, I would suggest mentioning this during your initial announcement. In my experience, when multiple companies are breached by the same threat group, people tend to be more sympathetic. It's less likely that they will see your company as being incompetent because it worked against multiple companies, and it is harder for people to justify saying all the affected companies were incompetent. So making a statement like "On September 1st 2020, we suffered a ransomware attack by xxxx threat group similar to the attacks against [company 1] and [company 2]" will make it easier for you to fly under the radar and seem more like an unfortunate victim than an incompetent company.

**Understand Your Business Partners' Needs:** When you're communicating with your stakeholders it's important to give them the information that they need. For example, if you are a third-party vendor to another company many times they need a statement from you saying that none of their customer PII has been leaked during the data breach. Consumers may be more concerned with things like their credit card numbers, social security numbers, name, addresses, and other things that would affect them directly.

**Don't Say Too Much:** You don't need to share the intricate details of your investigation with the public, this can lead to scrutiny of how you're performing your investigation. You only need to share the results of what you've found and in private you can consult with the experts you've brought in to ensure you are going about the investigation the right way.

**Offer Customer Protection:** In order to mitigate the loss of customers it's good to offer customer services like credit monitoring. It helps to reduce the impact of stolen information for your customers and shows them that you care about them, which makes them more likely to continue doing business with you.

## RECAP

In order to properly handle media communications during a Cybersecurity breach, you need to properly understand your notification requirements. These are local, national, and industry-specific. They outline who needs to be informed, set deadlines for when they need to be notified, and outline the acceptable means through which they should be notified. After an incident has occurred, it is important to provide regular updates, make yourself easy to contact, and try to minimize the impact of the data breach on customers and business partners.

# CHAPTER 19

# How to Handle Disgruntled Customers During a Data Breach

Whenever there is a major data breach, customers can be negatively affected. It's important that you handle your customers with care and provide them with the appropriate support to reduce the loss of customers that can often occur with major incidents. This chapter focuses on how to communicate with customers and support them to retain as many customers as you can.

We spent a lot of time in this book talking about the negative effects of a hack on the business but it's important to remember that customers can also have personal problems as a result of a data breach. The reason hackers want to steal customer information is because it is valuable. As a business, you want to accept responsibility for any data breaches you have and do what you can to help people that are negatively impacted as a result. First, let's look at some of the ways that people can be negatively impacted because of a data breach.

**Identity Theft:** Probably the biggest issue because of a data breach is identity theft. Hackers can use leaked information in order to take out loans in people's names, open lines of credit, impersonate people,

DOI: 10.1201/9781003264293-19

etc. This can lead to several issues that will affect customers for years to come. One of the biggest is a negative impact on consumers' credit history as lines of credit are opened in their names, which may go undetected for years and lead to bad payment history.

**Loss of Services:** If a business suffers a major hack this can lead to a loss of business operations for days, weeks, and even months, which can have a big impact on customers. For example, if you're a healthcare provider, customers can be in a very bad position if they can't get access to their services on time. Another big example of this is if you are some type of financial institution and people can't access their accounts when they need to.

**Invasion of Privacy:** Some of the information that is leaked or stolen may be personal information that people don't want others to know. For example, if you are a healthcare provider or an institution that deals with mental health, people don't want their history or treatment information to be available to the public and this can lead to damages to their reputation that may be impossible to resolve once it's been exposed.

As a business, your future can be decided based on how you handle your customers in this situation. You are going to have people that are upset with you for allowing this situation to happen and if you ignore them or fail to address their concerns, you can lose a lot of business. However, if you respond properly you can save a lot of business, retain loyal customers and mitigate the damages of a bad situation. In order to do this, there are a few core services that you can offer to customers that will make it easier for them to get everything they need from the business during the situation and they will appreciate you for making the effort to help them. Here are some of the services that I recommend you offer to your customers:

**Credit Monitoring:** Credit/fraud monitoring is probably the most important thing you can do to mitigate the risk to your customers following a major hack. When personal information is stolen, one of the biggest concerns of customers is that someone will try to steal their identity and ruin their credit score. Offering this service to people that are likely to be affected will be a great way to restore people's trust in the company.

**Provide Regular Updates:** Another thing you want to do is to control the narrative and keep people informed on what is happening. You don't want people's imagination running wild and them speculating on what was leaked, how bad the situation is, and what the company may or may not be doing. Use email, social media, and any applicable news outlets to keep your customers informed on what the situation is, and what has been leaked and reassure them that they are not at risk (unless you have good reason to believe that they are). One of the worst things you can do is to remain completely silent and let people speculate. You also want to make sure that customers know where to go to get updates or how to contact the company if they have an emergency situation as a result of the hack.

**Future Discounts:** Another good incentive to help keep people loyal to the company and compensate them for any time or money lost is to offer future discounts on company services. It's better to keep customers at a discount rather than lose them altogether. One good example of this is when Sony's PlayStation network went down for a few weeks/months, they offered all current customers free PlayStation Plus for months, which gave people an incentive to go back to PlayStation when the issue was resolved rather than switch to Xbox where they would have to pay a monthly fee for their online services. It would be a good idea to emulate this by giving customers a financial incentive to stay with the company despite this disruption to the business.

**Provide Alternative Companies:** If your company offers services that are essential to people, then you should have alternatives that your customers can use in the event that you ever have business disruptions. An inconvenience is one thing, but if you are a healthcare provider, financial intuition, or any other industry where you going out of business, it would have a serious impact on people's personal lives then you should have contingency plans for how you can get customers what they need in the event that your main infrastructure goes down. One way this can be done is by partnering with other businesses and having an agreement where you can use their services to fulfill your customers' demands on a temporary basis.

While you can do everything in your power to rectify the situation, it may be unavoidable that you will have customers that are upset and want to pursue some type of legal action. You should be prepared to respond to this and prove that your company did its due diligence to prevent this from happening. If this happens, it will require a collaboration between your legal team and your IT staff to show what actions the company took to protect your business and remediate the situation as soon as possible. Once you can prove that you did what was expected of you via the applicable laws and industry standards, then you should not have to worry about having to pay out any money to individual customers. Unfortunately, these situations can happen regardless of the security controls that you put in place.

## RECAP

Getting hacked is a stressful time for both the business and the customers alike. Hackers are very good at stealing consumer information and selling it to people that will use that information to commit identity theft/financial fraud via the dark web. This is one of the primary reasons why hackers want to steal consumer information. As a business, it is your responsibility and it's in your best interest to work with your consumers to mitigate the consequences of the data breach. If you fail to do so, you are going to lose a lot of customers and this will make it even harder for you to recover from the hack. In order to do this, you want to focus on providing your customers with a few different things. Firstly, offering credit monitoring services to help protect people from fraud is going to be huge in giving consumers confidence that this breach will not affect them financially. Secondly, you want to make sure that you consistently communicate with your customers and let them know what the status of the investigations is, what the potential effect on them will be, what you are doing to fix the situation, etc. The worst thing you can do once people find out about the data breach is to go silent and let people speculate on what is happening. Thirdly, you can offer future discounts in order to give people financial incentive to stay with your business and build rapport with your customers. Lastly, offer alternative means for your customers to get the services they need while you resolve the situation in order to minimize the negative impact on your customers.

# CHAPTER 20

# When Should I Get Law Enforcement Involved?

Whether or not to involve law enforcement when you have a data breach is a tough question. The scope to which they can get involved, the speed of the response, and the quality of expertise are all things to consider when deciding whether you should bring private consultants exclusively or ask for help from the police. This chapter evaluates the pros and cons of getting law enforcement involved and highlights when you have a legal obligation to report a data breach to the police.

ONE OF THE FIRST questions people have when they hear the scope of the cybercrime problem is why is no one stopping this? Given the amount of money companies lose, it should be a huge priority and typically it is. However, there are many complications that make it very difficult to prevent and catch people that are committing these crimes. Less than 1% of cybercrimes see a law enforcement action taken against the attackers, making it one of the hardest crimes to persecute [40]. Here are some of the main reasons why this happens:

1. **Legal Jurisdiction**: Since cybercrime occurs over the internet, a hack in the United States can be conducted by people in China, Russia, North Korea, and so on. The problem this creates is that the law enforcement of the United States may not have the authority to act in that country even if they have concrete evidence. They will have to

work with the law enforcement of the country that the person resides in, which can be a long tedious process that is only acted on if the crime is very severe. Also, consider that if the United States and the country at hand, such as North Korea, have bad relations; the situation becomes even more complicated and less likely to result in any type of arrest. Many people realize this and will conduct hacks in countries that don't have extradition rights in their home country and they can significantly reduce the chance of them being prosecuted.

2. **Global Scope**: The fact that cybercrime occurs on a global scale itself significantly increases the overhead and the amount of resources required to prosecute someone for a cybercrime. The process of tracking down where someone is in the world and then organizing the resources to go get that person is a large burden especially given the number of attacks that occur every day.

3. **Underreporting of Attacks**: Many companies simply don't report cyberattacks to the police when it happens. In 2016, the FBI's Internet Crime Complaint Center (IC3) estimated that only **15%** of victims actually report their cybercrime [41]. The main reason given was "what's the point?", given the difficulty of catching the criminals most people expect that nothing will happen and don't bother to report it.

4. **Gathering Evidence Is Difficult**: Courts and juries are well designed to handle traditional crimes. There's a good understanding of how evidence needs to be collected and handled and what the standard is for a conviction. However, with cybercrime, it can become pretty complicated and it's not something that most people are well versed in. Computer forensics, which is the scientific application of investigation and analysis to gather and preserve evidence from a computing device is a relatively new area. There aren't clear guidelines to prove that someone was responsible for a cybercrime. You need to be able to prove that the person in question was behind the computer and the one responsible for doing whatever actions they are accused of. Which requires you to find and correlate IP addresses, link that to a device owned by the user, and much more. Then, you must be able to convince a jury, despite the fact that most of them won't have a solid understanding of how computer systems work.

Based on the information given above, you shouldn't expect the police to be able to pick up your investigation and prosecute the average hacker. There are simply too many moving pieces that will make that difficult and most of the time it will not happen. However, there are some situations where it's worthwhile to get law enforcement involved.

**Insider Threats:** If you have a situation where someone within the company is suspected of aiding in a hack or tampering with your IT infrastructure, then this is a great time to get law enforcement involved. They don't have the hurdle of not having the person within their reach and they can easily bring that person in for questioning, conduct an investigation, and even press charges if need be. Just be sure to have your IT staff gather as much information as they can before you call them in so that they have enough evidence to pursue the matter and you should be good to go.

**Domain Squatting:** If you suspect someone of squatting on a domain that is attached to your copyright material, then you should contact law enforcement to help you get that domain taken down. You will need to file a UDRP complaint in order to have the domain provider take down the domain and this is something you need to file through law enforcement.

**Making Claims on Your Cyber Insurance:** If you want to make a claim through your cyber insurance, then you should make a police report so that there is a track record of what has happened and how much it has cost you. If the police are unable to help you resolve the situation, then you can take that report and go to your insurance provider as proof that you need to be reimbursed for the incident.

**Physical Damage to Your IT equipment:** One aspect of IT security that often goes overlooked is the physical security of your machines. If your servers are stolen or damaged by someone, you need to file a police report as soon as possible. Firstly, this is important if you want to make a claim on your cyber insurance as mentioned above. Secondly, there is a possibility that the police will be able to do an investigation and get your equipment back, which may be important depending on what information is on that machine.

## LAW ENFORCEMENT VERSUS PRIVATE CONSULTANTS

These are the most common situations when it may make sense to get the police involved but overall you want to keep a few things in mind when deciding if you should contact the police or a consulting company for help. If you are looking for help resolving the incident or guidance on how best to go about resolving the incident, you are better off contacting a consulting company that specializes in incident response. These companies deal with clients that have been hacked on a regular basis and are very proficient at helping companies through the crisis from start to finish. On the other hand, law enforcement is typically not going to help you through the actual resolution of a security incident; that's not what they are there for when it comes to cybersecurity. Consulting companies are more centered on helping you contain and resolve the attack while the police are more focused on helping to prosecute the people responsible. You will want to get the police involved when you are looking to prosecute someone or you need to have evidence that you have reported the incident, for example, if you are looking to make a claim with your insurance.

## WHEN DO YOU HAVE A LEGAL OBLIGATION TO REPORT A DATA BREACH TO THE POLICE?

Whenever you suffer a data breach, you have reporting obligations to different regulatory bodies and in Chapter 21, we are going to go in-depth on who you need to report to when you suffer a data breach. However, this section is focusing specifically on when you should be reporting a data breach to the police. For the most part, you will only need to report a data breach to the regulatory body that is responsible for that type of information but if you have any reason to believe that the information that is leaked could endanger someone's life or be used to cause serious harm to someone you should get the police involved. That's the biggest distinction between when you should report to the police vs simply reporting to regulators. If you're on the fence on if you should report a breach to the police or not I would recommend that you do it, it doesn't really do any harm to do so and it doesn't take a huge time investment either.

## RECAP

Unfortunately, due to the nature of cybercrimes, it is very difficult for police to prosecute most hackers. Since cybercriminals can launch their attacks from anywhere in the world, the amount of manpower it would take to pursue them and workaround different legal jurisdictions simply makes the effort not worth the offense in many cases. If you are looking for help in containing and recovering from a cyberattack, you are typically better off getting a private consulting company to assist you. If you are in a situation where you believe the person can be prosecuted, such as an insider threat or physical theft, you need a record of the incident or think someone's safety may be in danger, then you should report the situation to the police. Otherwise, you should focus on meeting all of your mandatory notification requirements to regulatory authorities.

# CHAPTER 21

# Public Authorities You Should Notify Throughout a Data Breach

This chapter will give a list of common public authorities that need to be notified in the event of a data breach. These authorities are usually dictated by the industry and location of the company as well as the country of citizenship of the customers whose information was stolen. There's a time limit on when these bodies need to be notified and failure to do so can result in additional fines, lawsuits, and even suspension of your business license. This chapter will inform readers of all of the regulatory bodies that they may need to be aware of.

For the final chapter of this book, we are going to outline whom you need to report to when you suffer a data breach. These authorities are typically the first people you should be reporting to when you suffer a data breach because of their strict reporting timelines. If you fail to do so, it can have very serious consequences. While the exact notification requirements will be determined by your company's exact circumstances (industry, location, size) there are some public authorities that have a prominent impact across the globe and those are the ones we are going to highlight here:

## US DEPARTMENT OF HEALTH AND HUMAN SERVICES

They oversee HIPAA, which stands for Health Insurance Portability & Accountability Act and was passed by Congress in 1996. The privacy aspect of HIPAA is overseen and enforced by the US Department of Health and Human Services (HHS) office.

## BREACHES AFFECTING FEWER THAN 500 INDIVIDUALS

HIPAA breach notification requires that healthcare providers notify patients in the event of a data breach that affects their information. The covered entity should also notify the Secretary of the breach within 60 days of the end of the calendar year in which the breach was discovered. You may report all of your breaches with less than 500 individuals on one day but you must complete a separate notice for each breach.

## BREACHES AFFECTING 500 OR MORE INDIVIDUALS

In the event that the breach includes more than 500 patients, the company must notify the secretary of the breach without unreasonable delay and in no case later than 60 calendar days from the discovery of the breach. If the number of individuals affected by a breach is uncertain at the time of the submission, then the business should provide an estimate and as new information is discovered, submit updates using the method below.

All notifications should be submitted to the Secretary using the web form found on the hhs.gov website.

**Information Commissioner's Office (ICO):** This is the regulatory body that oversees GDPR (EU General Data Protection Regulation) and it requires that businesses report personal data breaches that meet the criteria within 72 hours of the business becoming aware of the breach. To report the data breach you should call the ico.org helpline between 9 am and 5 pm. You can also notify the ICO using online reporting forms on their website. Under the definition of the GDPR, a personal data breach consists of the following [42]:

A breach of security which leads to the accidental or unlawful destruction, loss, alteration, unauthorized disclosure of, or access to personal data. This means any personal data that is stored, processed, or transmitted. It includes more than just losing personal data. Personal data breaches can include:

- access by an unauthorized third party

- deliberate or accidental action by a controller or processor

- sending personal data to an incorrect recipient (e.g., being sent to the wrong email address)

- devices being lost or stolen that contained personal data (e.g., laptops and mobile phones)

- alteration of personal data without permission

Only personal data breaches are considered data breaches for the GDPR. Therefore, the reporting obligations only apply to personal data. It also only applies to living people.

However, it's important to note that not all personal data breaches are required to be reported to the ICO. When a personal data breach occurs you need to evaluate the likelihood of negative consequences to the victims including financial, risk to people's rights and freedoms, emotional and physical distress etc. If you determine that it is unlikely for any negative consequences to occur then you don't need to report it but you will have to justify your decision so you should document the breach and why you came to that conclusion. Here are some of the things you should consider when making that evaluation:

- Sensitivity of data

- How easy it is to identify people from the data

- Potential consequences

- Severity

- How vulnerable is the person to fraud, manipulation, etc., due to this data breach

## REPORTING A DATA BREACH TO ICO

If you deem that a data breach should be reported to the ICO, you have 72 hours to do so after becoming aware and this includes evenings, weekends, and bank holidays. If you take longer than this, you must provide justification for doing so. When providing the report to the ICO be sure to include the following details:

- A description of the nature of the data breach. This should include how it happened, how many people it affected, and the type of personal data records that were leaked.

- The name and contact details of your data protection officer or other contact points. This person may be contacted to provide more information on the situation.

- A description of the likely impact and consequences for customers affected by the personal data breach.

- A description of the measures taken or proposed to be taken to deal with the personal data breach.

You also have the option of reporting the data breach in phases if you don't have all of the information available at the end of the 72-hour deadline.

## WHEN DO YOU NEED TO NOTIFY INDIVIDUALS ABOUT A DATA BREACH?

Depending on the situation, ICO may require you to notify customers directly. If a breach is likely to result in a high risk to the rights and freedoms of individuals, you are required to inform those that have been affected directly and without delay. The threshold for notifying individuals directly is higher than those for notifying the ICO itself. But it should be done in high-risk scenarios so that people can take steps to protect themselves from the effect of the breach.

**PCI-SSC:** In September 2006, five major credit card brands (Visa International, MasterCard, American Express, Discover, and JCB) established the payment card Industry Security Standards Council (PCI-SSC). PCI-SSC created and continues to oversee PCI-DSS (payment card industry data security standard), which is an information security standard for organizations that accept or process credit cards in any way. PCI-DSS is unique in that they don't have any nationwide notification requirement like other regulations have. They have no requirement for notifying the public or even notifying the PCI SSC. However, you do have a requirement to notify your payment processor, who will then share that information with the card companies. Outside of that, there is no international notification requirement for PCI-DSS but there may be local-level requirements so check them for your area.

**Office of the Privacy Commissioner of Canada (OPC):** This is the privacy office that oversees Canada's major data privacy legislation PIPEDA (Personal Information Protection and Electronic Document Act). The PIPEDA is a regulatory requirement that applies to private sector organizations that collect personal information in Canada (this includes countries that are headquartered abroad but have a real and substantial business presence in Canada). It's designed to ensure the protection of personal information in the course of commercial business.

## WHEN DO YOU NEED TO REPORT A BREACH?

PIPEDA requires that you report any breach of security safeguards that involves personal information under your control if you reasonably believe that this breach creates a real risk of significant harm to an individual.

The OPC defines significant harm as the following [43]: "includes bodily harm, humiliation, damage to reputation or relationships, loss of employment, business or professional opportunities, financial loss, identity theft, negative effects on the credit record and damage to or loss of property."

PIPEDA has also provided a list of factors that you can use to evaluate the real risk of significant harm, here are the two factors that they listed [44]:

**Sensitivity:** While PIPEDA doesn't give a definition of this, they give the example of things like medical records, income records, ethnic and racial origins, genetic and biometric material as well as an individual's sex life or sexual orientation. To best determine sensitivity you want to examine what information was breached and the circumstances around it. It also matters how easily this information can be leaked to an individual person.

**Probability of Misuse:** You want to evaluate how likely it is that someone will be able to use this information to harm someone, commit fraud, is there evidence of malicious intent, who could have accessed this information, etc.

Some questions you may wish to consider are:

- What happened and how likely is it that someone would be harmed by the breach?

- Who actually accessed or could have accessed the personal information?

- How long has the personal information been exposed?

- Is there evidence of malicious intent (e.g., theft, hacking)?

- Were a number of pieces of personal information breached, thus raising the risk of misuse?

- Is the breached information in the hands of an individual/entity that represents a reputation risk to the individual(s) in and of itself? (e.g., an ex-spouse or a boss depending on specific circumstances)

- Was the information exposed to limited/known entities who have committed to destroying and not disclosing the data?

- Was the information exposed to individuals/entities who have a low likelihood of sharing the information in a way that would cause harm? (e.g., in the case of an accidental disclosure to unintended recipients)

- Was the information exposed to individuals/entities who are unknown or to a large number of individuals, where certain individuals might use or share the information in a way that would cause harm?

- Is the information known to be exposed to entities/individuals who are likely to attempt to cause harm with it (e.g., information thieves)?

- Has harm materialized (demonstration of misuse)?

- Was the information lost, inappropriately accessed, or stolen?

- Has the personal information been recovered?

- Is the personal information adequately encrypted, anonymized, or otherwise not easily accessible?

## HOW TO SUBMIT A BREACH REPORT TO THE OPC AND AFFECTED INDIVIDUALS

The process for submitting a report to the OPC is simple, you can submit a breach report to the OPC using the "PIPEDA breach report form" [45] found on their website. When it comes to notifying affected individuals, there isn't one set method but you are required to notify any individual whose personal information has been leaked if you believe it creates a real risk of significant harm to the individual. You are required to notify them directly (telephone, mail, email, etc.) and it must be conspicuous (not overly legalistic and easily understandable). It should include enough information for the individual to understand the significance of the breach and to take steps to reduce the risk of harm to themselves. The notification to individuals must include the following information [43]:

- a description of the circumstances of the breach;

- the day on which, or period during which, the breach occurred or, if neither is known, the approximate period;

- a description of the personal information that is the subject of the breach to the extent that the information is known;

- a description of the steps that the organization has taken to reduce the risk of harm that could result from the breach;

- a description of the steps that affected individuals could take to reduce the risk of harm that could result from the breach or to mitigate that harm; and

- contact information that the affected individual can use to obtain further information about the breach.

Under PIPEDA, organizations are required to notify the Privacy Commissioner of Canada and affected individuals "as soon as feasible" whenever there is a data breach that has a "real risk of significant harm". You are also required to keep a record of each breach of safeguards involving personal information, regardless of if it is reported or has a real risk of significant harm. You are required to retain this record for at least 24 months.

## RECAP

Whenever your company suffers a data breach, you should be aware of what your notification requirements will be. This will be dependent on the compliance regulations that are applicable to your company based on your industry, location, and company size. While the exact notification requirements will vary depending on the regulatory body, there are some common things you should look for. Firstly, you need to understand what circumstances you are required to report a data breach. You may not be required to report every data breach you have, especially if it doesn't constitute any risk to the people whose information was leaked. Secondly, you want to understand what the deadline is for notifying the organization, typically this will be "as soon as reasonably possible" or within 72 hours of finding out about the breach. If you take longer, you will be expected to provide a reason for the delay. Thirdly, you need to understand the median by which you should notify the regulatory body as well as affected individuals. This can be through web forms, phone calls, email, mail, etc. Each regulatory body may have specific methods by which they want to be notified and require that you notify affected individuals. Lastly, you should understand what responsibilities you have when it comes to keeping a record of the incident. Some bodies require that you keep a record of all data breaches for as much as two years following the incident.

# Conclusion

THIS WILL BE A recap of all of the key points outlined within the book that readers should keep in mind as they implement these concepts in their business.

## TOP 10 KEY CYBERSECURITY CONCEPTS TO REMEMBER

### Personally Identifiable Information (PII)

PII is a broad term for any information that can be linked to an individual person and will usually be a combination of multiple individual pieces of information. Protecting PII is one of the most important aspects of cybersecurity. Whenever you hear about a company getting hacked and information being stolen, it's primarily PII that is being talked about and it's something that needs to be protected. The most valuable type of PII is a subset called personal health information (PHI). The reason it's so valuable is that criminals can use this PHI to commit fraud that will allow them to get access to medical equipment and or medicine that they wouldn't be able to get access to on their own. Once they obtain these medical resources, they can be resold for a good profit.

### Cyber Insurance

Second on this list is cyber insurance; this is a very cost-effective way of reducing the chance of your business going under because of a cyberattack. For less than $1500 a year, you can cover for several types of cyberattacks and their related consequences:

- Data destruction
- Extortion
- Theft

DOI: 10.1201/9781003264293-22

- Hacking

- Denial of service attacks

- Liability coverage for damage done to other companies

- Regular security audits

- Post-incident public relations

- Investigative Expenses

- Criminal reward funds, for example, paying ransoms

- Notifying customers about a data breach

- Credit monitoring for affected customers

Cybersecurity attacks aren't covered in traditional insurance policies, so it's important to look into getting insurance specifically for cyberattacks.

## The Principle of Least Privilege

This concept should be applied throughout your organization at all times. The assignment of excessive privileges is a huge risk in business and can be avoided by simply applying this principle. This simply means that any employees, contract, or third party should be given the least amount of access and information needed to do their jobs. Minimizing the amount of access and information that people have reduces their ability to perform actions that may be damaging to your business. It also limits the damage a hacker can do if they are able to compromise a legitimate user account.

## The Incident Response Lifecycle

In this book, we covered the National Institute of Standards and Technology's (NIST's) version of the incident response lifecycle. This is one of the most popular frameworks for handling and investigating security incidents and is used by many corporations as a means of standardizing the way they respond to security incidents. In this workflow, NIST recommends four steps: 1) Preparation, 2) Detection and Analysis, 3) Containment, Eradication, and Recovery, and 4) Post-Incident activity.

## Quantifying the ROI of Cybersecurity

One of the most important skills you will develop as a mid-senior level employee is being able to quantify the return on investment (ROI) of your cybersecurity programs. Remember cybersecurity is still a business unit and companies are only willing to invest in it because it either makes the company money or it saves the company money. In order to keep getting the higher-ups to invest in your team and your program, you need to be able to quantify the ROI that they are getting on every dollar invested.

There are four primary ways that a cybersecurity initiative gives you an ROI:

- Reducing business risk

- Compliance with regulations or contractual agreements

- Reducing ongoing costs

- Meeting business objectives

**Reduction in Business Risk:** This is the primary means that an investment in Cybersecurity will pay back a business. Anytime the company suffers some type of security breach, there is a cost associated with that. So by reducing the rate of occurrence for a specific type of incident, you save the company the money. For example, say Company A suffers 10 data breaches a year because of phishing emails that cost 10,000 to fix (10 × 10,000 = $100,000 per year). To fix this, you implement a security control that costs you $20,000 but reduces the rate of occurrence by half, saving you $50,000 per year. Your payback in the first year alone will be (50,000 − 20,000) $30,000. This is one way a cybersecurity initiative can have a measurable ROI, but looking at the annual rate of occurrence, calculating the expected decrease in the rate of occurrence, and subtracting the amount of the control. Controls can be technical things like a firewall but it can also be hiring additional staff to do training or to respond and contain the situations as they occur.

## Risk-Reduction ROI

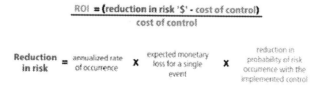

$$ROI = \frac{(\text{reduction in risk '\$' - cost of control})}{\text{cost of control}}$$

| Reduction in risk | = | annualized rate of occurrence | X | expected monetary loss for a single event | X | reduction in probability of risk occurrence with the implemented control |

**Compliance:** The next way Cybersecurity gives ROI is in the form of meeting mandatory compliance regulations. So there are two types of compliance regulations that apply in this situation, firstly you have government or industry regulations. These will vary depending on your location and the type of industry the company operates in. Secondly, you have contractual obligations, so if you're a service provider for another company there may be clauses in the contract that say you have to have certain things in place from a security point of view. Failing to meet either of these compliance regulations can result in a lot of negative consequences such as fines, loss of clients, lawsuits, and, in severe cases, imprisonment.

**Reducing Ongoing Costs:** This means finding ways to optimize the current security or business processes so that it reduces overall costs. Some examples of this include reducing the required storage space or reducing time and effort through automation. Typically, this will never be the sole focus of a security project but it's a good additional reason.

**Meeting Business Objectives:** Security is usually a part of IT and they often have specific business objectives that they need to meet. One of these objectives that overlap very heavily with security is availability. This includes things like recovery time objectives (RTO), recovery point objective (RPO), and having a certain amount of uptime. Any security project that is essential for or supports meeting business objectives is much more likely to get support and recognition from management.

## Security Simulations to Prepare for a Hack

The best way to know how prepared you are for a hack is to have someone try to hack you. Having routine security testing is very important for making sure that your organization's cybersecurity program is effective and that you are well protected from outside attacks. In addition to regular security testing like a penetration test or a vulnerability assessment you also want to test your company throughout the entire process of handling a cybersecurity incident. This means doing simulations from start to finish where you can assess your team's ability to respond to cybersecurity incidents. Here are some of the simulations you should consider doing.

**Tabletop Exercise:** A tabletop exercise is a discussion-based session that usually takes place in a conference room with upper management or executives. The purpose here is to look over the plan, use it in a few different theoretical scenarios, identify any gaps in the plan through brainstorming, and ensure all business units that will be needed are represented in the plan. It doesn't take much resources and can be done routinely without causing a big burden.

**Structured Walk Through**: In this type of exercise, each team member walks through their individual component of the plan in order to find any gaps. Usually, this is done with a specific type of situation in mind, for example, hurricane or earthquake.

**Simulation Testing**: For a simulation, you gather all of the personnel that will be involved in the response plan and go through a simulation of an emergency and see how well the plan functions in that situation. These should be done at least once per year.

**Parallel Test**: In this type of test, failover systems are tested to make sure that they can perform real business operations and support key processes and applications in the event of a disaster. Primary systems still carry the full production workload.

**Cutover Test**: This takes the parallel test further and uses the failover systems to support the full production workload. You completely disconnect the primary systems. This type of test gives you as close as possible to a guarantee that in the event of a disaster, your failover systems will be able to support your entire business.

## Remember Third-Party Risks

Another often-neglected aspect of cybersecurity is third-party risks. It's important that organizations take time to assess how their business partners could be a risk to their business either through the data that they hold or the access they have to your company's facilities and network. There are about three main risks that you have when dealing with third-party vendors.

**Network Security:** If another company has access to your network in an insecure way this can lead to your company getting hacked. By insecure I mean if there isn't proper network segmentation. For example, in a good network architecture, the company will have all of its servers that need to be accessed from outside the company network in a DMZ, which is separated from the internal network and prevents people from outside the company from accessing anything except the servers that are meant to be public. In an insecure network architecture, people will be able to access more than just the public servers from outside of the internal network, which can result in getting hacked. As we discussed earlier, getting hacked is typically very expensive to recover from and you want to avoid that at all costs.

**Regulatory:** This is where a third-party vendor that has your company's information is not compliant with one or more of the regulations that affect your company. You are ultimately responsible for ensuring that any third-party that you share information with is being handled in compliance with the applicable regulations. Not being compliant may result in fines or require you to suspend your business operations if it's a serious offense. Generally, this information should be shared with your third-party vendors during the onboarding process and you should have them sign a contract agreeing to handle your company's data in the correct manner.

**Operational:** This would be any disruption to your company's operations where you're unable to provide products or services to your customers. A common example of this would be if you're using a cloud provider. If the server that's hosting your website goes down unexpectedly that means your customers will not be able to access your website and that will cost you business. If your company has a business model like Netflix that requires high uptime then this can be catastrophic to your business.

## Compliance and Notification Requirements

One underlying theme in this book is the connection between cybersecurity and your compliance regulations. Most of the major compliance regulations such as GDPR, PIPEDA, or HIPAA all require certain levels of security for data protection. It's your job to understand what the security requirements are to satisfy these regulations. Here are some of the main ones you want to keep in mind:

**PCI-DSS:** PCI-DSS stands for payment card industry data security standard. In September 2006, five major credit card brands (Visa International, MasterCard, American Express, Discover, and JCB) established the Payment Card Industry Security Standards Council (PCI-SSC). PCI-SSC created and continues to oversee PCI-DSS, which is an information security standard for organizations that accept or process credit cards in any way. Failure to comply with the rules outlined in this standard can result in heavy penalties. For example, one Tennessee-based retailer was charged $13.2 million by Visa for failure to meet the standards. Typically, fines range from 5k to 10k per month until compliance is achieved, but these fines increase the longer a company doesn't meet compliance. Also, fines ranging from $50 to $90 can be charged per affected customer if a data breach occurs.

**CCPA:** The California Consumer Privacy Act (CCPA) gives California residents more control over the personal information that businesses collect on them. CCPA applies only to for-profit businesses that do business in California (regardless of where your headquarters is) and meet any of the following requirements:

- Have a gross annual revenue of over $25 million.

- Buy, receive, or sell the personal information of 50,000 or more California residents, households, or devices.

- Derive 50% or more of their annual revenue from selling California residents' personal information.

It doesn't apply to non-profit businesses or government agencies.

CCPA fines a maximum civil penalty of $2500 for every unintentional violation and $7500 for every intentional violation of the law.

**GDPR:** GDPR stands for General Data Protection Regulation and it is a privacy law set out by the European Union (EU). It became effective as of May 25th 2018. Even though it was set out by the EU, it affects all companies that collect information for citizens of the EU. Ernst & Young estimated that the world's 500 biggest corporations are on track to spend up to $7.8 billion on GDPR compliance. As of January 2020, GDPR has led to over $126 million in **fines**, with the biggest fine being 50 million euros paid out by Google. GDPR fines **up to €20 million ($24.1 million) or 4% of annual global turnover** (whichever is higher).

**HIPAA:** HIPAA stands for Health Insurance Portability & Accountability Act and was passed by Congress in 1996. The privacy aspect of HIPAA is overseen and enforced by the US Department of Health and Human Services (HHS) office, starting in April 2003. HIPAA does a few different things, but from a compliance point of view, it's all about mandating the protection of consumer health information, this is referred to as HIPAA privacy regulation. HIPAA privacy regulation requires health care providers and their business associates to develop and follow procedures to ensure the confidentiality and protection of PHI. You can see HIPAA fine information below.

**PIPEDA:** The Personal Information Protection and Electronic Document Act (PIPEDA) is a regulatory requirement that applies to private sector organizations that collect personal information in Canada. It's designed to ensure the protection of personal information in the course of commercial business. Compliance requires that you follow 10 fair principles that govern the collection, use, and disclosure of personal information as well as providing access to personal information for customers. PIPEDA fines include up to $100,000 per violation.

**SOX Compliance:** SOX stands for Sarbanes–Oxley Act, passed in 2002, and it establishes regulations to protect the public from fraudulent business practices by corporations. It was passed following some large business scandals, where companies like Enron, Tyco, and Adelphia used deceptive business practices to trick the public. In order to protect consumers, it mandates more transparency in the financial reporting of corporations. It requires companies to have formalized checks and balances to ensure that their reporting is accurate. SOX applies to all publicly traded companies in the United States, subsidiaries, and foreign companies that are publicly traded and conduct business within the United States.

When it comes to penalties and fines, SOX specifically penalizes the corporate officer (usually CEO or CFO) that is responsible for compliance. An officer that doesn't comply or submits an inaccurate certification is subject to a $1 million fine and ten years in prison, even if done accidentally. If an inaccurate account is submitted on purpose the fine can be up to $5 million and 20 years in prison.

**Australia Data Privacy Act:** In 1988, the privacy act was passed and serves as Australia's primary piece of legislation for protecting the handling of personal information about citizens of Australia. This act applies to all government agencies and private sector organizations that have an annual turnover of $3 million or more. The privacy act is supported by the privacy regulation of 2013 and the privacy (credit reporting) code of 2014.

## What Do You Need in an Incident Response Team?

When building out an incident response team there are certain roles that need to be filled in order to be effective and to be sure that you can respond to any situation that arises. While you can have one person fill multiple roles within a team it's important that you have every capability covered. Here are the roles that you want to ensure that you have on your team:

**Team Leader:** This is a person or people that will be responsible for coordinating all of the incident response team's activities. For this role, the person doesn't need to have a lot of technical expertise but they should be good at communication and project management. This person may also be responsible for reporting any important information to the proper stakeholders within the company.

**Communications:** Next, you need someone that can handle communication with outside stakeholders. For example, let's look at data privacy. If you have a security incident that compromises the privacy of a customer's information then that needs to be reported to the appropriate data privacy office. You need someone either on your team or working with the team that can be a subject matter expert on these issues and make sure that you are meeting all of your communication requirements. In addition to communicating with outside stakeholders, you also want someone that can handle all internal communications within the business. You may need to inform employees of a cyberattack or other internal emergency and you don't want your IT staff doing that, you want someone who is trained in communications that knows how to tailor the message and control the narrative to create these messages. Lastly, in the event of something like a ransomware attack, where you need to communicate with hackers and potentially negotiate on behalf of the company, you want someone with expertise in communications to handle that negotiation.

**Technical Investigator:** This serves as the technical expert on the team. When you're doing an investigation you may need to do things like examine log files, do computer forensic work, or extract evidence from a system using security tools. The technical investigator/expert is someone that excels in doing this type of intensive, technical work and can provide support for other analysts where needed. This information will be used to determine the cause of the attack, signs of compromise, lateral movement, and other important indicators in the security incident.

**Analysts/Investigators:** Now these are people that are going to do the bulk of the work for your incident response team. Typically, the way this works is that you have multiple analysts and as potential security incidents come in, they are assigned to individual analysts that will run those investigations and keep the team leader informed on what's happening. These analysts need to have a strong foundational knowledge of cybersecurity as well as the incident response lifecycle so that they can be counted on to run the investigations properly. For very technical components of the investigation, they can leverage the technical investigator for those tasks.

**Legal Counsel and HR:** This may not be apparent at first but you should have legal counsel and someone that is familiar with HR practices consulting the team. While most of your security incidents will be from external threats, insider threats are still a real risk and you're going to need people that can advise you on your internal investigations. For example, you need to know how to handle employees that are suspected of foul play in case you want to press charges, fire them, etc. Legal counsel will be important for informing you of employees' rights as well as the rights of your customers while HR is important for helping to deal with employees.

**Data Privacy:** Whenever there is a successful hack, you run the risk of customer data being compromised. There are several laws both local and international that give customers right over the data that has been collected by a business. In that situation the business needs to take steps to ensure that they are in accordance with those laws, inform the proper people and take the steps required to fix the situation. This person may or may not be separate from the legal counsel. Sometimes, your company may have a lawyer that specializes in data privacy or they will have someone who is a data privacy specialist.

Defense in Depth

The last item on this list of the concept of defense in depth. This is going to be important for setting up your company's network. This is the idea that any important network resource should be protected by multiple layers of security. In the same way you want redundancy for your network resources, you should not have a single point of failure when it comes to the security controls that you use to protect your network. Not only should you have redundant security controls but you should implement different types of controls that cover different aspects of security. Some common examples of this would the three following areas:

1. **Physical Controls:** This includes all tangible/physical devices that are used to prevent or detect unauthorized access to company assets. This means things such as fences, surveillance cameras, guard dogs, and physical locks and doors.

2. **Technical Controls:** This includes hardware and software mechanisms that are used to protect assets from non-tangible threats. This includes things like encryption, firewalls, antivirus software, and intrusion detection systems (IDS).

3. **Administrative Controls:** This refers to the policies, procedures, and guidelines that outline company practices in accordance with security objectives. Some common examples of this will be employee hiring and termination procedures, equipment and internet usage, physical access to facilities, and separation of duties.

## FINAL THOUGHTS

This book is meant to be an all-in-one guide on what to do when you get hacked. This process begins before the hack even starts, if you fail to prepare before a hack happens it will be very difficult to recover from a cyberattack. It begins with proper planning so that you have the proper people, processes, and technology in place to ensure that you can respond effectively to whatever happens. While this book doesn't cover every situation that you could potentially run into, if you implement what is in this book, your cybersecurity will be solid and prepared to handle the vast majority of situations that you will run into during the lifespan of your business. However, as technology and the world continue to change, what you need to protect your business from online threats will also continue to change. To help with this, I've put together a list of online resources, most of which are free that you can use to stay up to date on what's happening within cybersecurity and to build out your own cybersecurity program as technology continues to change.

## AVAILABLE RESOURCES

**Securitymadesimple:** This is my personal blog, it's a website dedicated to teaching cybersecurity to business owners and giving advice to people interested in getting into the field. Here, I write on several topics, including many of the topics I've written about in this book in more detail. That blog will be regularly updated with new content and it's a good place to get information as things in the industry continue to change. Here, you can find a ton of articles on different cybersecurity topics that would be valuable to a business owner.

**OWASP:** The Open Web Application Security Project (OWASP) is an online community that produces freely available articles, methodologies, documentation, tools, and technologies in the field of web application security. If you're someone that is working on a web application or your company is built around a web application(s), this is a great free resource to help you learn how to secure that application.

**NIST:** The National Institute of Standards and Technology (NIST) is a physical sciences laboratory and a non-regulatory agency of the United States Department of Commerce. Its mission is to promote innovation and industrial competitiveness. They have tons of cybersecurity-related standards and documents that can help guide you on how to protect your company. As we discussed, one of their best resources is their detailed incident response lifecycle guide that can help you plan out your company's incident response plan.

**HackerOne & Bugcrowd:** These two platforms are good places for setting up bug bounty programs if you want to get your company's applications, environments, or websites tested. Both of these websites are free to use and give you access to hundreds or if not thousands of capable security researchers that will expose weaknesses in your company's infrastructure.

**Department of Defence CISA:** This stands for Cybersecurity & Infrastructure Security Agency; they release information on many different areas related to homeland security including cybersecurity. If there are any really big cybersecurity attacks affecting multiple companies, they may release advisories on what you can do to prevent them. If you're a company that works for the federal government, then you can find even more resources for your business here.

**SANS Institute:** SANS is mostly known for its cybersecurity training but they also offer free templates for a lot of different types of cybersecurity policies. This way you don't need to come up with the whole document yourself, you can take pieces from these templates knowing that it comes from a reputable source. Additionally, it is well known for its extensive training programs for security staff, and is therefore a great place to consider sending your staff for training on the latest tools and techniques for cybersecurity.

**Canadian Center for Cyber Security:** This website is hosted by the Canadian government and they give tips on cybersecurity for small businesses as well as overall cybersecurity awareness for the community. If you live in Canada or work for a Canadian government agency, you get even more access to training, education, and security assessments for your business.

**Secjuice:** This is the only non-profit, independent, and volunteer-led cybersecurity publication to date. It is a publication entirely focused on information security with an emphasis on hacking, network security, and open source intelligence. It's a great website to follow for information on the industry as well as technical tutorials related to cybersecurity software.

**Helpnetsecurity:** This is another great publication dedicated to cybersecurity. They create great content on cybersecurity news and threats. They have a large team of writers that have many years of experience; so their breakdowns are usually very thorough and very informative, which is great for an InfoSec professional that is looking to stay informed on the latest in the industry.

# Sources

[1] https://cybersecurityventures.com/hackerpocalypse-cybercrime-report-2016/

[2] https://www.cybintsolutions.com/cyber-security-facts-stats/

[3] https://www.thirdway.org/report/to-catch-a-hacker-toward-a-comprehensive-strategy-to-identify-pursue-and-punish-malicious-cyber-actors

[4] https://www.fbi.gov/news/stories/ic3-releases-2016-internet-crime-report

[5] https://www.ibm.com/security/data-breach

[6] https://cybersecurityventures.com/60-percent-of-small-companies-close-within-6-months-of-being-hacked/

[7] https://www.cybintsolutions.com/cyber-security-facts-stats/#:~:text=Share%20prices%20fall%207.27%25%20on,post%2Dbreach%20according%20to%20Comparitech

[8] https://purplesec.us/resources/cyber-security-statistics/

[9] https://www.siliconrepublic.com/enterprise/ransomware-palo-alto-networks-report-h1-2021

[10] https://secure2.sophos.com/en-us/content/state-of-ransomware.aspx

[11] https://www.newyorker.com/magazine/2021/04/26/the-incredible-rise-of-north-koreas-hacking-army

[12] https://www.privacyaffairs.com/dark-web-price-index-2020/

[13] https://www.preferreditgroup.com/2019/08/27/the-three-goals-of-cyber-security-cia-triad-defined/

[14] https://comodosslstore.com/blog/what-is-digital-signature-how-does-it-work.html

[15] https://digitalguardian.com/blog/whats-cost-data-breach-2019

[16] https://www.cnbc.com/2021/08/10/main-street-overconfidence-small-businesses-dont-worry-about-hacking.html

[17] https://advisorsmith.com/cyber-liability-insurance/cost/

[18] https://www.varonis.com/blog/gdpr-effect-review/

[19] https://www.reuters.com/article/us-google-privacy-france-idUSKCN1PF208

[20] https://seedscientific.com/how-much-data-is-created-every-day/

[21] https://threatpost.com/retailer-stands-pci-racket-031213/77618/

[22] https://www.varonis.com/blog/pci-compliance/

[23] https://securiti.ai/blog/ccpa-fines/

[24] https://www.securitymetrics.com/blog/how-much-does-gdpr-compliance-cost

[25] https://www.cnbc.com/2020/01/19/eu-gdpr-privacy-law-led-to-over-100-million-in-fines.html

[26] https://www.varonis.com/blog/gdpr-effect-review/

[27] https://www.hipaajournal.com/what-are-the-penalties-for-hipaa-violations-7096/

[28] https://essextec.com/wp-content/uploads/2015/09/IBM-2015-Cyber-Security-Intelligence-Index_FULL-REPORT.pdf

[29] https://insights.sei.cmu.edu/blog/handling-threats-from-disgruntled-employees/

[30] https://www.hrdive.com/news/careerbuilder-74-of-employers-admit-hiring-the-wrong-candidate/512577/

[31] https://www.securityweek.com/facebook-paid-22-million-bug-bounty-rewards-2019

[32] https://www.axxys.com/blog/dont-operate-business-one-day-without-backup-recovery/

[33] https://blog.knowbe4.com/bid/252429/91-of-cyberattacks-begin-with-spear-phishing-email

[34] https://www.techrepublic.com/article/why-23-of-companies-never-test-their-disaster-recovery-plan-despite-major-risks/

[35] https://www.the20.com/blog/the-cost-of-it-downtime/#:~:text=According%20to%20Gartner%2C%20the%20average,hour%20at%20the%20higher%20end

[36] https://www.linkedin.com/pulse/how-test-your-business-continuity-disaster-recovery-shimon

[37] https://www.darkreading.com/attacks-breaches/top-15-indicators-of-compromise

[38] https://securityboulevard.com/2020/02/third-party-risk-management-best-practices-for-protecting-your-business/

[39] https://www.theamegroup.com/security-breach/

[40] https://www.thirdway.org/report/to-catch-a-hacker-toward-a-comprehensive-strategy-to-identify-pursue-and-punish-malicious-cyber-actors

[41] https://www.ic3.gov/Media/PDF/AnnualReport/2016_IC3Report.pdf

[42] https://www.rocketlawyer.com/gb/en/quick-guides/data-breach-reporting

[43] https://www.priv.gc.ca/en/privacy-topics/business-privacy/safeguards-and-breaches/privacy-breaches/respond-to-a-privacy-breach-at-your-business/gd_pb_201810/#_Part_1

[44] https://www.priv.gc.ca/en/privacy-topics/business-privacy/safeguards-and-breaches/privacy-breaches/respond-to-a-privacy-breach-at-your-business/gd_pb_201810/#_Part_6

[45] https://www.priv.gc.ca/en/report-a-concern/report-a-privacy-breach-at-your-organization/report-a-privacy-breach-at-your-business/

# Index

Printed in the United States
by Baker & Taylor Publisher Services